Praise for
A MODERN PROF.
ANSWERS YOUR KEY QUESTIONS ABOUT LIFE

"A compassionate, understanding, immensely helpful response to the spiritual, emotional, and practical problems that
confront ordinary people at the end of the twentieth century. The
question-and-answer format helps the reader to identify with
the issues raised, and makes the answers seem directed at one
personally—a most engaging and sparkling production!"

—Robert S. Ellwood,
Emeritus Professor of Religion,
University of Southern California
Coauthor, *Religious and*
Spiritual Groups in Modern America

"A highly recommended book filled with practical, spiritual
nuggets for transforming our lives."

—Gerald G. Jampolsky, M.D.
Author, *Love Is Letting Go of Fear*

"This book offers a wealth of spiritual information and analysis,
which is both illuminating and comforting."

—Michael Newton, Ph.D.
Author, *Journey of Souls*

"Harold Klemp is a pioneer of today's focus on 'everyday spirituality'."

—Arielle Ford
Author, *Hot Chocolate for the*
Mystical Soul

"This is a book that brilliantly combines the esoteric wisdom
of [the] East and West for today's needs in life, love and learning.
Harold Klemp's insights place him among the most esteemed
spiritual leaders of our time."

—Rosemary Ellen Guiley
Author, *The Miracle of Prayer* and
Dreamwork for the Soul

"Now [that I am] at more than four score years [of age], so many previously unanswered questions are, for me, comfortably resolved in *A Modern Prophet*. The specters of doubt and anxiety are diminished with prescient and spiritually sensitive answers for a person of any age, religion or race. And it's all in one volume, spelled out in depth and focused clarity."

—Edith S. Engel
Compiler and Editor,
ONE GOD: Peoples of the Book

"Harold Klemp takes you on a guided tour of your inner self by answering questions which will help awaken you to your own God-given abilities."

—Taylor Hay
Author, *Synergetics*

A
MODERN
PROPHET

ANSWERS YOUR KEY
QUESTIONS ABOUT LIFE

Also by Harold Klemp

Ask the Master, Book 1
Ask the Master, Book 2
Child in the Wilderness
The Living Word, Book 1
The Living Word, Book 2
Soul Travelers of the Far Country
The Spiritual Exercises of ECK
The Temple of ECK
The Wind of Change

The Mahanta Transcripts Series
Journey of Soul, Book 1
How to Find God, Book 2
The Secret Teachings, Book 3
The Golden Heart, Book 4
Cloak of Consciousness, Book 5
Unlocking the Puzzle Box, Book 6
The Eternal Dreamer, Book 7
The Dream Master, Book 8
We Come as Eagles, Book 9
The Drumbeat of Time, Book 10
What Is Spiritual Freedom? Book 11
How the Inner Master Works, Book 12
The Slow Burning Love of God, Book 13
The Secret of Love, Book 14
Our Spiritual Wake-Up Calls, Book 15

Stories to Help You See God in Your Life
The Book of ECK Parables, Volume 1
The Book of ECK Parables, Volume 2
The Book of ECK Parables, Volume 3
Stories to Help You See God in Your Life,
ECK Parables, Book 4

MAHANTA

This book has been authored by and published under the supervision of the Mahanta, the Living ECK Master, Sri Harold Klemp. It is the Word of ECK.

A

MODERN PROPHET

ANSWERS YOUR KEY
QUESTIONS ABOUT LIFE

HAROLD KLEMP

ECKANKAR
Minneapolis

A Modern Prophet Answers Your Key Questions about Life

Copyright © 1998 ECKANKAR

Printed in U.S.A.

Compiled by Mary Carroll Moore
Edited by Joan Klemp and Anthony Moore
Text illustrations by Ann Hubert
Back cover photo by Robert Huntley

Library of Congress Cataloging-in-Publication Data

Klemp, Harold.
  A modern prophet answers your key questions about life / Harold Klemp.
    p. cm.
    ISBN 1-57043-143-4 (alk. paper)
    1. Eckankar (Organization)—Miscellanea.   2. Spiritual life—Miscellanea. I. Title.
BP605.E3K56455 1998
299'.93—dc21   98-24225
                                                  CIP

♾ The paper used in this publication meets the minimum requirements of the American National Standard for Information Sciences—Permanence of Paper for Printed Materials, ANSI Z39.48-1984.

CONTENTS

INTRODUCTION

When you travel the road to God, you venture into uncharted territory. Sometimes a crossroads will appear: Which direction do you take? Decisions made in the smallest parts of your life can affect the success of your journey.

How do you decide? Is there anyone who has been there before and can answer your questions?

The sincere seeker of truth often finds that his real questions go without an answer and his inner experiences with the Light and Sound of God are not explained. Where can he find someone who has already traveled the road to God—and come back to tell about it?

Harold Klemp is one such person. He is a modern-day prophet. As the spiritual leader of Eckankar, he gets thousands of letters from seekers of truth around the world. All want direct and useful answers about how to travel the road to God. Harold replies personally to many of these letters with insights and advice from his own experience.

The teachings of ECK define the nature of Soul. You are Soul. You are like a star of God sent into this world for spiritual experience. That will purify you.

Karma and reincarnation are thus primary beliefs in ECK. Your goal in this lifetime should be spiritual freedom. After that, you become a Co-worker with God, both here and in the next world.

Key to the ECK teachings is the Mahanta, the Living ECK Master. He indeed acts as both the Outer and Inner Master for ECK students. The prophet of Eckankar, he is given respect but is not worshiped. He teaches the sacred name of God, HU. When sung just a few minutes each day, HU will lift you spiritually into the Light and Sound of God—to the ECK (Holy Spirit). This easy spiritual exercise and others will purify you. You are then able to accept the full love of God in this very lifetime.

Sri Harold Klemp is the Mahanta, the Living ECK Master today. Author of many books, discourses, and articles, he teaches the ins and outs of the spiritual life. His teachings lift people and help them recognize and understand their own experiences in the Light and Sound of God. Many of his talks are available to you on audio- and videocassette.

In this book are over two hundred questions and answers to help you.

Topics he covers are many. Among them are the value to you of spiritual exercises, self-discipline, and planning versus surrender. They tell how to avoid making karma, the roles of divine love and human love, what our children and pets may teach us, how spiritual healing really works, how to love God, and more. *A Modern Prophet Answers Your Key Questions about Life* is a valuable guide to help you find a life of joy, service, and contentment.

Ponder upon these topics. You will benefit at every stage of your journey home to God. Now, get set to read and learn more about you.

To find out more about the author and Eckankar, please turn to pages 273–78 in the back of this book.

Dreams are like a daily report card. They show you how you are doing in your spiritual mission, even if you don't know you have one.

1
DREAMS

What is the purpose of dreams?

There is a spiritual side to every experience or event, no matter how large or small, and whether or not it occurs in everyday life or in a dream.

But—and this is a big *but*—few people have the spiritual eyes to see.

Most people are in a daze but don't know it. They have hardly any idea about their life in the higher spiritual worlds while their body lies asleep at day's end.

Dreams are like a daily report card. They show how you are doing in your spiritual mission, even if you don't know you have one. Dreams tell how you are getting on in your relationship with God and life.

Dreams tell how you are getting on in your relationship with God and life.

ARE DREAMS REAL?

Are the people and places in my dreams real? Are other people having the same dream as I am?

A dream is a real experience. As Soul, a spiritual being and a divine spark of God, you can (and do) have hundreds of experiences going on side by side at different levels. So does everyone else.

Here is a way to understand the variety of inner experiences: it's as if Soul experiences what hundreds of people in a town do on a certain day. The mind, meanwhile, can recall only a few experiences at a time.

You may remember a certain inner experience with someone on the inner planes because of its spiritual importance for you. However, the other person will likely remember a completely different experience, because your needs are different.

In comparison to Soul, our mind holds only a few memories at a time. We remember those that mean the most to us spiritually.

Only rarely do the spiritual needs of two people exactly coincide. When they do, both dreamers will remember the same dream. However, their different levels of consciousness will give each a special view of what actually happened in the dream state.

In comparison to Soul, our mind holds only a few memories at a time.

WAKING OR SLEEPING

What does the dream state represent that the waking state does not?

There is no difference in my mind. Each person is Soul, capable of being fully aware twenty-four hours a day. The lessons of life come to us every minute, on every level. However, few people today pay much mind to the power of Soul and Its being. The average person goes through life with only the barest sense of his or her true identity as Soul, a spark of God.

Why can't I be aware of all my dreams? Why do I forget them after I awaken in the morning?

There can be any number of reasons. The physical mind is limited, like a little bucket. The inner experiences you have on all the spiritual planes are like a vast ocean. It is useless trying to pour the ocean into the mind's little bucket.

Soul is running several bodies at the same time on other planes. Its scope of action is much greater than the recall ability of the dreamer's mind.

Sometimes the mind wants to protect you because the dream would shock you. It's a different world with different rules. You wake up here, and right away this world crowds in on you. And you say, "I've got to get up, go to work."

START REMEMBERING YOUR DREAMS

I wish I could remember my dreams better. Can you help?

Some people naturally enjoy vivid recollections of their dream state, but those who don't can develop the skill.

You can set a dream in your mind before you wake up by repeating the main points of it, then talking about it out loud or writing it down as soon as you wake up.

It is also possible to develop a sharper recall of the dream state by keeping a notebook by the bed, with pen and light at hand. Make a resolution to wake—even in the middle of the night—to record any memory of the dream state, no matter how trivial it seems.

What are your dreams like?

I no longer refer to my Soul journeys as dreams. In the past, yes, I did dream.

It is also possible to develop a sharper recall of the dream state by keeping a notebook by the bed, with pen and light at hand.

Now my journeys into the spiritual worlds are crystal clear, without the sense of distortion so common to dreams. That's why I prefer to call my dreams Soul journeys. But I do study an inner event and try to see what message it might hold for my waking life.

How do you interpret your dreams?

There are key dreams (I'll call them dreams) that tell me about problems at work. One group of such dreams has to do with baseball.

If the playing field in the dream is in top condition as at a major-league stadium, then all is well. Usually it's not. The location of the field might be partly in a woods and partly in a cow pasture. The bases are at odd distances from each other and often out of sight. It means something in my daily life is not in balance, and I'd better find out where and how the situation got so out of shape.

There are key dreams (I'll call them dreams) that tell me about problems at work.

A Spiritual Dream

I had a dream in which I was walking down a sidewalk with a friend at 9:00 p.m. I looked up in the sky and saw the moon, which looked huge. Beside the moon was a big planet with a ring around it. Everyone else in the dream seemed to take no notice but carried on as if it were just an ordinary day. I was excited and wanted to know why the moon and planet were there. Can you please explain to me what this dream means?

Yours is a spiritual dream.

The sidewalk is your spiritual path in life. Since it's your dream and your path, the lessons will be yours—not your friend's. Evening means the end of Soul's karmic day: this life is your gateway to spiritual freedom. Looking up into the sky indicates your high spiritual vision. The huge moon is the promise of a brighter life, here and now.

The big planet with the ring is a symbol for the great spiritual worlds beyond our own. You alone, of all the others in the dream, were thrilled at the sight of the moon and planet because of your appreciation for spiritual things.

DREAMS WITHIN DREAMS

Sometimes when I am dreaming, I wake up to find I am still dreaming. And I wake up again to find myself waking up in yet another dream. I have counted as many as fifteen or twenty of these awakenings before I am awake in my physical body. What is this experience?

This is an excellent sign of your spiritual growth.

You, as a spiritual being, as Soul, can run a number of bodies at one time. During the process of waking up, Soul is returning from these far places, and you may momentarily remember each of your inner experiences or inner bodies in turn. By the time you wake up here, your attention is completely nested in your physical body again for everyday life at school, work, or home.

The multiple awakenings show your developing growth in the worlds of God.

I was having a dream about one thing, and some other dream jumped in and interrupted. In fact, about five different dreams did that. I was dreaming about being in a pasture and then some ninjas jumped

You, as a spiritual being, as Soul, can run a number of bodies at one time.

out and attacked me. What does this mean, if anything? Why do dreams do that?

Dreams do not really jump in on each other at all. What happens is that in the Soul body you are jumping from one inner experience to another.

Soul can be in several different places at the same time. This is not unusual, because Soul runs at least one body on each of the lower spiritual planes, and sometimes more. What you see as skipping from one dream to another is like switching TV channels to see what programs are on. Such skipping about gets old, so we usually settle down to watch whatever interests us the most, like your dream of the ninjas.

Your experience with the ninjas in that dream world was real. When we watch violence on TV, it means we are in agreement with it inwardly. This opens us to nightmares. It's better to watch happier programs or read uplifting books if we want more restful dreams.

The dream world and its people are real. It is only our recall and understanding of it that are incomplete.

Is It Real, or Is It a Symbol?

How can I tell whether the people I meet in the dream state are other Souls or just symbolic parts of myself?

The dream world and its people are real. It is only our recall and understanding of it that are incomplete. Our link with the inner worlds is usually through dreams, but illusion can make our memory of inner events faulty.

What about the dream people who appear to be just symbolic parts of ourselves? Let's start with what I call the waking dream. The Mahanta uses it to give someone a spiritual insight from an experience in his daily life. The Mahanta is an expression of the Spirit of God that is always with you. This inner guide draws on the individual's experiences with real people and real events to point out some personal truth.

Apply the principle of the waking dream to your dream world. The people you meet there are Souls, just like you. However, the Mahanta can turn your experiences with them into an open window of understanding, to unlock your desires, needs, and goals.

PROTECT YOURSELF FROM NIGHTMARES

Apply the principle of the waking dream to your dream world.

I am twelve years old. I had a bad dream where I was attacked by the negative power in the form of a bad character from a cartoon on TV. I would like to know how to avoid frightening dreams like that in the future. Thank you.

To avoid frightening dreams caused by a certain cartoon on TV, watch other cartoons instead. Don't let anything into your life that hurts or frightens you, if you can do something about it. That means not just a cartoon show, but also people, food, habits, etc. You'll be much more at peace with yourself.

DREAM TESTS

In a dream I saw myself in a class that looked like an auditorium. After class, one of my friends and I went up to the teacher, who said he could only give truth to people thirty-three years of age or more. Since I was fifty, I told him I qualified. Others in the dream later gave me encouragement.

In a second dream, a so-called holy man brought gifts to my two friends and me. They took them, but I did not. What do these dreams mean?

In the first dream, the teacher was a spokesman for the Mahanta. The teacher set an artificial qualification of acceptance: he would accept no one younger than thirty-three years of age. It was an easy qualifier, which fit your age. But you yourself had to state, "I am qualified to learn truth." It is Soul's commitment to the ways of Divine Spirit.

The second dream was to test your sincerity. Were you really ready to follow God or was this just another spiritual shopping trip? You refused the lesser gifts, even though your friends accepted them, because you desired only the gifts of God.

The second dream was to test your sincerity. Were you really ready to follow God or was this just another spiritual shopping trip?

YOUR DREAM SWORD

In a dream, I had left my body and was flying. I was holding a sword that gave me a lot of energy and made me feel like a child. It was guiding me. When I let go of it, it was as though I lost the energy and began falling back toward my body. Eventually I didn't have to hold the sword anymore but just had it by my side.

The sword is your mantra, your secret word.

The Mahanta puts energy into your secret word and makes it what it is. Once this inner guide establishes power in your word, one more thing is needed to make it work: your attention. Thereafter this word can lift you into the secret world of dreams. Your secret word connects you with the ECK, the Holy Spirit, which then guides you everywhere. However, should your attention lapse, the dream comes to a swift end and you reenter the body.

With practice, your word becomes so much a part of you that you sing it in time of need without a second thought.

FEAR OF DEATH IN DREAMS

I have had a recurring dream ever since I was a child. I'm taking a bath, and a hand falls into the tub and grabs my toe. I usually wake up screaming, very scared and having trouble breathing. What does this dream mean?

Your dream about a hand falling in the bathtub and grabbing your toe is, oddly enough, a spiritual dream. It shows a deep fear of dying, even though outwardly few people would guess that of you.

Taking a bath sets the dream up as meaning: Be ready; this is a spiritual dream. For water often means something spiritual. Being in the bathtub means you're immersed in thoughts of a spiritual nature. But then the hand falls into the tub. It's not a normal hand, but a *disembodied* one. *Disembodied* here means death. The hand grabs your toe, the very end of your body. That means, "In the end death will get you."

Once you understand that this is a spiritual dream, you will find its power over you will lessen.

Your dream shows a deep fear of dying, even though outwardly few people would guess that of you.

DIRECTION IN LIFE

I dreamed I was in a car and I was eating, paying no attention to the fact that the car was driving very safely on its own. When I noticed that the car was moving, I thought, Boy, am I lucky to have the Mahanta taking care of me. *I then decided to take control of the car and drive it myself. When I did this, the seat moved back so I couldn't reach the steering wheel and the windshield got all foggy. I barely kept from hitting a truck.*

Yours is a very good spiritual dream. The car,

of course, is your life. Eating means doing the spiritual exercises and living the life of ECK (Divine Spirit).

Anyone who does the Spiritual Exercises of ECK finds his life runs very well because the unseen driver is the Mahanta, this expression of the Spirit of God that is always with you. You know this. Trouble begins when one sees how well things are going and then takes credit for it. That's the ego getting behind the wheel. The seat moved back means that the ego and mind are too far away from spiritual control (the steering wheel) to be able to run things right. The foggy windshield means the clouded vision of the ego, or the human self.

Dreams give a personal look at where you are now in your spiritual unfoldment. The Mahanta uses them to tell the spiritual student how well he is unfolding. Write down your dreams and study them. They will give you all the direction in life you need.

Dreams give a personal look at where you are now in your spiritual unfoldment.

What can dreams tell us about ourselves?

Dreams hint at truth. I say *hint* instead of *tell* for a reason: Most people don't actually want to know the truth. The truth hurts. Dreams can tell us when we're unkind, unfair, vengeful, selfish, and other unpleasant facts that we need to work on spiritually. But truth makes most people uncomfortable, so they shut it out and forget their dreams.

I've tried many dream systems and have kept a record of my own inner travels for years. Of all the systems, the dream methods of Eckankar are the golden thread that have been of the most use to me for spiritual growth.

SENSATIONS OF FALLING

I used to have an experience that I wish you would explain. Whenever I was waking up from sleep, I would feel as though I were falling from a great height and as if I were out of my body. I was never afraid because I felt familiar with the vibrations of those heights. What was most interesting was the beautiful music I always heard. Often I heard madrigals, with mostly female voices.

When you were waking up, Soul was coming back to the body from the higher planes. This gave you the feeling of falling from a great height and was a Soul Travel experience.

Hearing the madrigal indicates Soul Travel on the mental level of heaven, the Mental Plane, since this form of song particularly develops the mind. The madrigal is another expression of the Holy Spirit there, in addition to the sound of running water. This experience shows you are being prepared for the high spiritual planes in this lifetime.

When you were waking up, Soul was coming back to the body from the higher planes.

SHARING DREAMS

My wife and son had a dream the same night about the same subject. Both were bitten on the foot: my wife, by snakes; my son, by a monster. Is it possible to share the same dream? And what does it mean in the dream state to step on things like animals or to lose one's shoes? I've had dreams about misplacing my shoes and cannot start an important activity until I find them.

Two people can indeed share the same dream, especially when there is a close affinity between them. To your wife, the snake bites mean to watch

Two people can indeed share the same dream, especially when there is a close affinity between them.

for hidden or missing clauses in contracts that pertain to the building and furnishing of your new home. Watch for "snakes in the grass." The monster biting your son means for him to be aware of more obvious accidents around the home, such as the one he suffered recently. If attention is put upon the Spirit of God, these minor irritations can be avoided, for they need never be more than that.

To step on things like animals means to be careful not to hurt the feelings of others by thoughtlessness. The image of animals, which are often thought to be inferior to man, means a lack of sensitivity to those on the perimeter of our own consciousness.

Misplaced shoes or articles of clothing that prevent one from keeping important appointments mean that one's inner life has outpaced his outer life.

Misplaced shoes or articles of clothing that prevent one from keeping important appointments mean that one's inner life has outpaced his outer life. He must immediately set new goals in his daily life. This is so both worlds are brought into balance again; otherwise, he will be left with a gnawing feeling of misplacement. I hope this gives you an idea of how one approaches the interpretation of dreams.

SOUL'S FREEDOM

In a dream I walked up into some hills, and it seemed like the Fourth of July. Thousands of people were sitting on the hillsides looking into the sky as if expecting fireworks. The sky was light blue and free of clouds.

I walked past the crowds until I was alone again and looked at the hills in the distance. They were like hard-packed sand dunes without vegetation. Suddenly, a flash of red went by and stopped long enough for me to recognize it before disappearing. It was me. That made me feel really odd. Looking out over the ridge of hills, I saw that they had undergone a drastic change. They were much lumpier, and a huge boulder with green vines all over it had been raised ten feet into the air.

The dream felt very real. I had just gone through a doorway and was expecting a member of an ancient American race that I had just read about in a Louis L'Amour novel. But I woke up before he arrived.

This is what your dream means: Your walk up into the hills indicates that in the dream you were moving into a higher state of consciousness.

The Fourth of July is Independence Day for Americans. This image evokes the ideal of spiritual freedom, which you can achieve in this lifetime if you set your heart upon it.

The thousands of people are your collective awareness—i.e., the sum total of your thoughts and hopes. You are awaiting the ecstasy of spiritual freedom. When you leave the crowds, it means you leave behind your worries and come to rest in Soul, the center of your being.

You are now in the Soul body and look back on the hills, which are nothing more than events in your daily life. From the lofty vantage point of Soul, your outer life seems to be a spiritual wasteland, especially when you let anger (the "flash of red") flare up.

The image of the boulder is used in a double sense here. First, Soul studies the ridge of hills to see what harm anger might do, and It perceives a "much lumpier" life. Anger makes mountains out of molehills, or in this case, a huge boulder is raised ten feet into the air.

Second, green vines clinging to the face of the boulder show the power of envy or jealousy to undermine a relationship. Have you heard the phrase "green with envy"? The roots of the vines can, in time,

Your walk up into the hills indicates that in the dream you were moving into a higher state of consciousness.

shatter the greatest boulder, just as envy and jealousy can destroy the closest relationship, even one that seems "solid as a rock."

The member of an ancient American race whom you were expecting was the Mahanta, the Living ECK Master.

This dream gives a most exacting look at yourself to help you better understand yourself.

How can one explore other parts of oneself in the dream state?

A person is spiritually of six parts: the Physical, the Astral (emotions), the Causal (memory of past lives), the Mental (thought), the Etheric (intuition), and Soul (the eternal).

There is a sacred word for each level. For example, if you want to look at a past life, the word to sing for a few minutes at bedtime is Mana (say mah-NAH or mah-NAY).

It often takes a month to see a past-life experience, so don't give up the first day. You must have a very strong desire to see your past.

If you want to look at a past life, the word to sing for a few minutes at bedtime is Mana (say mah-NAH or mah-NAY).

FAMILIAR DREAM WORLDS

I would like to know the meaning of déjà vu. Recently, I have quite often been struck by pictures or remembrances of things I have already seen or lived. Could it be that I dreamed my entire life before?

Déjà vu is a strong feeling of already having experienced something before.

Life is a dream from beginning to end. Some people, like you, have the unusual ability of bringing the memory of a dream into the present moment. That is the reason so many things are already familiar to you. It is a special ability, but remember that other people have their special gifts too. That's why this world is such an interesting place to live.

Preparing for Your Future

I had a dream in which I found myself in a meeting in a city to which I will be moving. There was only one person there that I knew, and he was acting very out of character. The atmosphere was disturbing. Nothing was getting accomplished because people were interrupting each other and not paying attention. The meeting decayed, and I left.

Then I went through the city to the waterfront, where I walked along the water on a narrow boardwalk. Suddenly a storm blew in, and the water began getting rough, rocking the boardwalk. I realized I would probably be thrown into the water, and sure enough, the whole walk was soon overturned by the waves. The boards flipped over me and pinned me under the surface.

I relaxed, telling myself I could probably work myself free. But I tried and couldn't. Then I panicked, heaving up to try to reach air. As I strained frantically, I awoke in bed in a cold sweat.

No person, place, or thing is perfect. Keep this in mind when you move to the new city. The way of doing things there will certainly be different from what you are used to now.

How easy it is to mistake "different" for "wrong." We get caught up in our own ideas of right and wrong. If we become self-righteous on top of that, we find we are less tolerant in a new place, and everything seems to line up against us. Certainly, the last place most of us think to look for the cause of our grievances is inside ourselves, but that is usually the exact

The last place most of us think to look for the cause of our grievances is inside ourselves, but that is usually the exact source of our problems.

source of our problems.

Go to your new city with an open mind. What sense is there in trying to change everyone else in your new circle of friends when it's so much easier to change ourselves? Intolerance hurts us every time.

There is nothing in this dream you can't handle.

Dreams about Ancient Times

I haven't been having any dreams that I can remember for the past month. This is unusual for me; I usually have dreams all the time. Is it karma? I would like to know, if possible, because I learn from my dreams.

Another thing I would like to know is are there knights on the inner planes? I am attracted to medieval wars and battles.

In answer to your first question: By the time you read this, you will have started to dream again. There are times when Soul shifts gears; this is when we don't always remember our dreams. But it is a passing thing.

There are times when Soul shifts gears.

About your attraction to knights and medieval wars and battles: Your interest in that period of history is due to your many past lives there. It was a time of great adventure, chivalry, and heroics. The forces of darkness and light were in a hotly contested battle for centuries, and you played a part in those unsettled, but interesting, times.

History can teach us much about how mankind's unlearned lessons repeat themselves. This allows us to use our knowledge to avoid unnecessary problems, because we can sidestep a lot of them.

People make history. You might enjoy the four historical novels of Mary Stewart about Merlin that bring to life the times of King Arthur at the beginning of the Middle Ages: *The Crystal Cave, The Hollow Hills, The Last Enchantment,* and *The Wicked Day.* You'll find many spiritual insights in these books, for in them she is adept at looking at past-life records on the Causal Plane. The books are in the library.

REMEMBERING INNER EXPERIENCES

Is there anything I can do to help me remember experiences that I have inwardly?

You could write things down, but that's a hard way to do it. Sometimes you don't feel like writing. Another way to remember is to study the details of the experience while it's happening.

For instance, if you're at a baseball game on the inner, you could study the uniform of one of the players on the other team, see what kind of shoes he's got—cleats or whatever—and what color shirt he has on. Even notice the stitching on parts of the shirt.

Become aware of the little details. Notice a tree, a cat—and the cat's ears, how he twitches them. This exercise will help you remember dreams.

LEARNING NEW LAWS

I have always trusted my dreams and made most of my decisions based on them. I have had several dreams recently that did not manifest the way I dreamed them. This is a great crisis for me. Please help me find the truth.

Why can you not trust your dreams any longer? You're being taken to a higher level of understanding life: by seeing, knowing, and being. The Mahanta no

Why can you not trust your dreams any longer? You're being taken to a higher level of understanding life: by seeing, knowing, and being.

longer lets you lean on dreams to make judgments about others. That means you are now put in a position of looking at a person objectively.

From now on it means that trust comes first on your part. On the other hand, the other person is given a chance to earn that trust. You decide on the worth of a person because of what he actually does, not what you think he might do wrong.

Go ahead and learn all you can about the spiritual laws of this new level. They are certainly different from those you knew before. But you'll get the hang of it before you know it.

Serving Others in Dreams

I have had several dreams where I am talking to groups of people about Eckankar. In one dream I held a roving microphone for others to ask you questions. In the past people have told me that I have helped them in their dreams. I would appreciate some insight into this. Am I, as Soul, really doing these things?

The dream censor is quite protective of the emotional states and will garble the past-life experience in order not to upset the individual.

It was good to hear that you are remembering some of the service you are able to give on the inner planes. To many, this would be beyond comprehension.

When the individual first steps on the path of ECK, he generally confronts past-life experiences that emerge in the dream state through symbols. The dream censor is quite protective of the emotional states and will garble the past-life experience in order not to upset the individual.

So many who ask for remembrance of these experiences are actually receiving protection while certain karma works itself out by having scenes blotted from memory.

As one unfolds spiritually, the inner experiences become less phenomenal. Soul is gradually being led from the phenomenal worlds toward the worlds of true being at the Soul Plane and beyond.

Yet, some feel unhappy when they no longer have the experiences that date back to their spiritual childhood. It is like a high-school student demanding to become a first grader again because he was happier then. Life always takes us forward if we will go.

The Gentle Way of Dreaming

I am having difficulty with my dreams because I cannot stop worrying over details of my physical life. Please, I need your help.

Put forth every effort to learn and grow during the lessons of the day with a light attention on the presence of the Spirit of God.

The point is: Carry out the physical duties and responsibilities as if you're doing them for God.

Do the Spiritual Exercises of ECK as you usually do them, but at bedtime give a thought request to the Mahanta, with love and goodwill in the heart center: *I give you permission to take me to wherever you see I've earned the right.* Then go peacefully to sleep without giving all this another thought.

You can vary the phrasing every few weeks for the benefit of the mind, which likes the stimulation of new ideas.

Sometimes we try too hard and push against the doors of Soul, forgetting that the doors open inwardly and cannot be forced. The spiritual exercises work best if one can fill himself with love and goodwill by thinking of someone who makes him happy.

As one unfolds spiritually, the inner experiences become less phenomenal.

The spiritual exercises work best if one can fill himself with love and goodwill.

This gentle technique can bring one to a conscious awakening in the dream state.

THREE STEPS FOR BETTER DREAMING

What instruction, advice, or technique would you give someone on how to sleep properly, so he can make use of the period when his body is stilled and leave it to travel in the upper regions with his teacher?

There are three main steps I recommend on the path of ECK. First, arrange your schedule to get as much sleep as needed to be fresh in the morning.

Go to sleep as usual, but leave the eye of Soul alert to the coming of the teacher.

Second, for a few minutes before sleeping, read from any of the ECK books to signal your intent to pursue spiritual activity during sleep.

Third, contemplate upon the face of the Mahanta, the Living ECK Master at bedtime. Do this in either a seated position or lying on your back. In the spiritual exercise, give an invitation to the Inner Master like this: I welcome you into my heart as into my home. Please enter it with joy.

Then go to sleep as usual, but leave the eye of Soul alert to the coming of the teacher. Look for me, because I am always with you.

What the spiritual student does develop is the inner link with the ECK, the Holy Spirit. Thus he taps into the Supreme Creative Force that guides him around all the blocks in his path that once defeated him.

2
SOLVING PROBLEMS

I'm seventy years old, and I've been on the path of ECK for several years, but I haven't had what I'd call spiritual experiences. No doubt I am very much in need of God, but I haven't found It yet. I'm afraid I will not learn about heaven until I die.

I appreciate your sincere concern about the lack of spiritual unfoldment.

First, understand that not everyone is conscious of his experiences on the spiritual planes while living in the physical body. The curtain must be drawn across the memory at certain times in order for the individual to retain a balance in this physical world. Others are quite aware of the ECK, the Sound and Light of God.

There is a way some may develop their memory of their dreams by keeping a notebook and pen at the bedside. But it takes a remarkable amount of self-discipline to rouse oneself from a deep sleep, turn on the bed lamp, and scrawl down notes for ten to fifteen minutes in a cold room. Not everyone is up to it.

There are times a block in our spiritual lives prevents us from entering the next spiritual plateau.

There are times a block in our spiritual lives prevents us from entering the next spiritual plateau.

It is possible to do a fast of some sort to remove this block. Not everyone is able to do this, and it should always be done with the advice of a physician.

Here's what I did: When the dream memory stopped for a period of time, new efforts in a new direction were necessary to break through. I would go on a juice fast for a day, then regular food the next day, then juice again for the following day—and alternate between solid food and juices for several days. But I never did it too long at first, since our health is not always able to withstand the strain. This is an individual matter that I cannot recommend unless your doctor says it is all right.

I would also address myself honestly and ask: What do I want out of my spiritual study? Our motives must be pure.

The inner experiences are not to be used to lord our supposed spiritual greatness over others. Nor to brag about them. What do we want these experiences for?

Quite frankly, not everyone is ready for the spiritual life. That is all right. In ECK we are concerned with our personal relationship with the Holy Spirit and with God. One person may need phenomenal experiences, while another may not. Some have written that the flashy experiences are not what they want, but merely the seeing, knowing, and being that comes when one enters the higher worlds and becomes established there in consciousness.

There were times when it seemed that the Spiritual Exercises of ECK had stopped working for me. Looking back, I realize it was generally for one of two reasons: I had overstepped some spiritual law, such as the Law of Silence, or my spiritual life had entered one of its periodic quiet stages. The con-

Quite frankly, not everyone is ready for the spiritual life. That is all right.

scious and the unconscious states often alternate. When it was quiet, I worked on the virtue of patience; for the impatient person certainly will never find God.

If you're able to find any help to break through the spiritual blockage by something written here, I would appreciate hearing from you. It is Divine Spirit that assists us on the inner planes and not the personality of even the Living ECK Master.

I thank you for your concern with this situation and recommend that you experiment freely with the spiritual exercises that are found in the ECK works.

WHY DO TROUBLES COME?

Can you explain why we have problems?

Troubles that come to us are for our purification. They come to us because we must learn a divine law.

Divine Spirit will use the most negative situations to teach us, and we wonder, *Why has God forsaken me?* God has not forsaken us. We are unwilling to give up certain passions of the mind and take the next step in our spiritual development. Habits fall away once Soul decides It really wants spiritual realization more than Its vices.

The spiritual life is not meant to finally end the succession of problems, for they are given as opportunities for Soul's unfoldment. What the spiritual student does develop, however, is the inner link with the ECK, the Holy Spirit. Thus he taps into the Supreme Creative Force that guides him around all the blocks in his path that once defeated him.

One's ability to take charge of his own life increases. This is a solid step toward self-mastery and

Troubles that come to us are for our purification. They come to us because we must learn a divine law.

that state of consciousness called the kingdom of heaven.

Be Kinder to Yourself

I am going through some hard times, and I feel so alone. I am only fifteen, but I am not sure I want to live here on earth. What's wrong with me?

You are a special person who has a lot to give others, but you've got to learn to be kinder to yourself. There's no school that teaches that, of course, but you can strike an attitude of openness as to how that can come to be.

If you have quiet conversations with yourself, ask, How can I be kinder to myself? Asking will open a door. Watch for people who live a life of kindness to themselves and others. For now, don't try to copy them—just watch.

If you have quiet conversations with yourself, ask, How can I be kinder to myself? Asking will open a door.

Believe me, a lot of people much older than you don't know what to do with their lives. But there are people who act with kindness. Watch for them, and you'll find exactly the kind of life you're looking for. But you'll have to work for it. We all pay our dues.

Why Troubles Equal Unfoldment

Lately I have been through a very lonely time where sadness has been a frequent visitor. When I realized that the way back to God was mine to travel alone and that I couldn't even talk about some of these things with my husband, the pain was intense.

The troubles we face are only for our own unfoldment. Our trials are difficult for us, but they mean little to our neighbor. He has his own troubles.

The way becomes narrower, but as our self-discipline to do those things that help us along the path increases, we discover that life can no longer defeat us. We move tranquilly under the protection of that Presence we know as the ECK, the Holy Spirit.

Our service to God, then, is given in the little things of life. The joy of spiritual awareness that now lights up our consciousness puts discouragement aside.

Each problem we control makes us greater in the eyes of God and one step closer to self-mastery.

ATTITUDES CREATE YOUR WORLD

Why don't troubles go away once we ask for help?

Much of the trouble we have in life is a result of some long-standing negative attitude. It has created these situations. Soul gains experience as It works through these rough spots on the road.

Some of our troubles will be dispelled by Divine Spirit while others are not. They are part of the divine plan for Soul to gain the purification or change in consciousness so It can know what It is. It needs to know why It has reincarnated into today's family and business environment.

Many people do not understand that life, with its burdens, is a treasure. The weight of disappointment makes us close our eyes to the gift of being in the world to learn about the loving heart.

Our service to God, then, is given in the little things of life.

RISING FROM FAILURE

I am depressed over the condition I find my life in. I cannot even look for a job because I am afraid I would just be bored with it, and I am not able to face another failure. What can I do?

Sit down and list the things you like and do not like about yourself.

Sit down and list the things you like and do not like about yourself, in separate columns. Look at them once a month. As you review the past thirty days, look for any changes the Holy Spirit has brought to you.

Self-discipline is an absolute necessity if one is to have a productive life. Replace old tastes and preferences with new, better ones. But do it in the name of God, with love and a sincere heart, or nothing will come of this experiment.

You must also look at how you wish to spend your time at work. Plot out a rough plan for getting (and holding) a job that has the things in it needed to keep your interest. Take care of the outer needs of the body because they are important for a sense of well-being. What you want to do is live the complete life.

The Spiritual Exercises of ECK build up spiritual momentum for Soul to realize the godlike being that It is; therefore, it is imperative that you do them for a twenty-minute period every day. If you have the discipline for that, I will certainly be with you at all times.

LACK OF HARMONY WITH OTHERS

A friend is always trying to draw me into her conflicts. How do I handle this problem, since she is very close to me?

There are people who try to draw others into their problems. Their own troubles are overwhelming because they like the attention from others.

Of course, how much you choose to become a part of her world is for you to decide. But don't feel guilty if you want to pull out of the situation because it interferes with your life.

She has to make up her own mind about personal decisions. If her inner guidance gives her a direction, fine. All her decisions have to be her own.

You may act as a listening post if you want to. But don't let her take your life away from you.

HOW PROBLEMS CHANGE AS YOU GROW

As I go along on the path of ECK, my problems seem to get bigger, yet I am able to handle them better. Can you explain this?

As you grow spiritually, you're forced to address problems that the average person wouldn't even dream existed. Once you wade through the cobwebs and dig out a solution, the same kind of problem-solving can be transferred to the next difficulty that comes along. We can learn to be on top of things instead of being the reactive victims.

As you grow spiritually, you're forced to address problems that the average person wouldn't even dream existed.

The only thing that keeps me plugging along in the face of difficult situations is that in the high worlds of ECK there is no time or space. Therefore, our detours are only so much learning. There is no point in getting somewhere faster or slower, sooner or later. God cares only that Soul is perfected sometime in Its wanderings. Nobody is in a hurry.

How can anyone get lost in the worlds of God? Such a thing is not possible. We've all done our share of racing ahead and sliding back in our lives. After all, that is the way of nature here—a constant back-and-forth motion that ends in maturity.

SOUL'S LOVE FOR GOD

What really causes all the problems I have in my life?

This connection may or may not make sense to you, but many of the things that have caused you problems are Soul's desire to love God.

When one feels unable to receive such love, life is meaningless. I wish I had words to say this better.

When you ask for help, the ECK, the Holy Spirit, begins to bring changes that are for your good. Of course, this means you must be extra careful in the choices you make. Before Spirit can make any changes, you must develop a better image of yourself: You are Soul. God's love is for you.

THE ROAD TO GOD

My life is filled with money problems and other kinds too many to enumerate. I am asking you for guidance so I can go on. I want to understand how to solve these problems. I also want to gain the understanding to allow the Holy Spirit to really express Itself in my life.

You are Soul. God's love is for you.

All problems come from the inner to the outer; therefore, we want to find out what is being done on the inner planes that is bringing about the problems out here, which seem to be too much to endure at times.

There is no need to run through clichés such as "There is no such thing as an accident," "All that befalls us is for a reason," or similar sayings. But what is causing all the trouble in terms that can be understood and accepted? And what is the solution?

The individual must be honest with himself and ask, *What did I expect from the spiritual path when I took up the ECK teachings?* The path to God is the path to God. It is not an easy one, otherwise many would be on it.

Life is truly meeting ourselves. The complaints

we have of others are reflections of our own deficiencies. It makes no sense to patch up our spiritual life with Band-Aids. The teachings of ECK are to give us a deep spiritual healing that touches all aspects of our lives. It's not done with a magic wand, however. Has one kept up the spiritual exercises, not with the robotic diligence of a person using prayer beads, but with a real desire to open himself to the secrets of God?

There are two basic paths for one to take in the lower worlds in an effort to find God—the path of love or the path of power. Most opt for power. This direction is the breeding ground for all the ills that come from the five passions of the mind. Life is for him a disaster, and he wonders what keeps him from taking an easy way out.

Love is the only way to God. The only way.

Love is the only way to God. The only way. If you want to go this route, ask the Mahanta in contemplation to be shown the way. The individual's heart must be pure in this request. There must also be a complete surrender to the Spirit of God. No holding back or having opinions of what is right or wrong about what is given to light the Golden Heart. The ECK is real but Its altar must be come to with humility and love, if one is to ever see Its ways.

In 1975, I got myself in a very unbalanced situation where I thought I was losing my mind. I lost my job and my wife, and my whole world crumbled because of this. Somehow I had drastically thrown my emotions out of balance. Although the pain has healed, I am still very much blocked up inside. I ask you with all my heart: Is there some way out of this condition for me?

I greatly appreciate the concern you expressed about your spiritual life. The question is really,

How do I open myself to life and still stay in balance?

Frequently, when one inadvertently opens himself to the spiritual forces before the proper preparation has been made, there is a great series of upsets in personal affairs. This could have been avoided had one known earlier to go slow on any spiritual path: avoid reading too many spiritual books or spending too much time in contemplation.

This is not a criticism, for most of us at one time or another have found ourselves in the same predicament.

The first step to rebuilding our inner worlds is to put some attention here on the physical state of our personal life. Get our business straightened out. Get it together down here on earth. Then gradually and cautiously move out again into those areas of the spiritual things we did not fully understand before and met with in a collision.

The first step to rebuilding our inner worlds is to put some attention here on the physical state of our personal life.

Sometimes, surprisingly, one's nutrition is lacking. This is often best approached through help with a competent, licensed medical doctor.

Take it easy and don't rush. Guidance can be found inside yourself. It will often come with a gentle nudge to perhaps seek out a doctor or a certain book that is beneficial to you at that particular time.

WHY IS YOUR LIFE HARD?

I would like to find some love and happiness in my life. But I am in such a muddled state of confusion that I feel I can't get out. I am absolutely broke and exhausted, out of energy to keep going. What am I missing?

Sometimes our life is hard because we make the wrong decisions. Why do we do that? Is it because we're afraid of something? Whatever the reason, this failure has been with us for years.

The teachings of ECK are about us being willing to change our state of consciousness to something better. Unless we agree to such changes, as offered by the Holy Spirit, they won't come. In fact, they cannot come. Ever.

Everyone on earth has problems. But most people do what they can to create a better life for themselves and their loved ones.

The key words here are *loved ones*. One must be able to love in order to have loved ones. Does anyone have a magic wand that can give love to a closed heart? I don't think so. Hearts are open for a reason, and closed hearts are closed for a reason. They don't just happen. Their owners must take responsibility for them, whether they are open or closed. Who else can be responsible if not the owner?

When you're making a decision about something, look at more than the benefits you'll get by doing it, whatever it is. Also look at what price it requires of you. Weigh *both* the benefits and the price before you decide whether to act or not.

Before you can improve your life and find a measure of happiness, you must learn to do one thing every day out of pure love.

Before you can improve your life and find a measure of happiness, you must learn to do one thing every day out of pure love. That means, don't expect anything in return—neither thanks nor happiness. Pick that occasion carefully. Then, whatever that one act of giving of yourself to someone else is, do it with all your heart.

You need to learn to give, without ever thinking of a reward. That's how to find the treasures of heaven.

What's the secret of staying in balance?

The secret of a balanced life is to live each

moment in the right spiritual frame of mind.

When something appears to go wrong, look for the lesson in it for you, instead of finding fault with anyone else or even yourself.

INNER HARMONY

I am very interested in a book by Whitley Strieber called Communion *and enclose a copy for you. In reading this and other books like it, I am concerned about keeping in balance. Is reading books such as this a sidetrack to my spiritual life?*

I would very much like to thank you for sending me *Communion* by Whitley Strieber. It is an area of great interest for a good many people. So little is generally known about alternate states of consciousness as they show up in other beings that inhabit our universe.

An interest such as this can become an all-consuming pastime, so that we end up missing the opportunities of our own spiritual advancement.

We don't want to get drawn into *anything* to that degree. The spiritual results are too limited.

Each of us is like a power station. We generate energy all the time, energy that can either build or destroy.

HOW TO AVOID UNCONSCIOUS KARMA

Can we create karma in our dreams? If so, how? And how can we avoid it?

Yes, people can create karma in the dream state. Yet most are unaware that they do so, even as they are unaware of karma they make every day.

Each of us is like a power station. We generate energy all the time, energy that can either build or destroy. If we let unworthy thoughts or desires leave our power station, they pollute everything around us. That is bad karma. Our mind is like a machine, able to issue contaminants around the clock. Our thoughts even run on automatic at night, when we may unconsciously try to control others or harm them in the dream state.

The problem is a lack of spiritual self-discipline.

To avoid making karma, while either awake or asleep, sing HU. It is an ancient name for God that people from any walk of life can sing. Sing it when you are angry, frightened, or alone. You can do this quietly within yourself or out loud. HU calms and restores, because it sets your thoughts upon the highest spiritual ideal.

When You See Your Future

In a recent dream I saw a situation which I understood to be a possibility in my future. Although I would eventually welcome it, I know that I am not ready for such a big step now. So I wonder why this would reveal itself to me at this time?

Dreams prepare us for the possibilities of our future.

Dreams prepare us for the possibilities of our future. A young girl may dream of becoming a wife years before she's ready for such a role. Later, her ideas may swing away from her youthful dreams of marriage, and new ones replace them.

But when the time comes for marriage, she is ready. She is ready to step into the role of a marriage partner with more love and confidence than she would have had as a girl. This is so because of her dreams.

Our dreams simply prepare us for many future possibilities. We can then decide which future path we want to go for.

BALANCING THE BLUES

*Around November and December, I am often filled
with negative feelings. What causes this?*

Your feelings are partly caused by the atmosphere that precedes the holiday season. However,
nothing is insurmountable for Soul; It learns how
to make everything into stepping-stones instead of
stumbling blocks.

The holiday season generates a lot of negative
energy as people find they are unable to buy the
presents they would like. Also, the gifts they *do* buy
are often beyond their means. A wave of this psychic
energy sweeps the world every Christmas. It is especially noticeable in crowds, as people hurry to do
their last-minute shopping.

This negative wave can color our own feelings
and make us despondent for no real reason. But
of course, the mind can always think of reasons
to separate itself from the Light and Sound of
God.

*The mind
can always
think of
reasons
to separate
itself from
the Light
and Sound
of God.*

Some people who have raised themselves above
the human consciousness are uncomfortable when
exposed to extremes of worry, scurry, and turmoil
during Christmas shopping. It is a lot like the swim-
mer who dives into ocean waters with fins, mask,
and snorkel. He can stay underwater only as long
as his lungs can hold the oxygen. So we sometimes
run into stores and leave fast.

HAVING PATIENCE

*I worry a lot about my spiritual progress. Should
I be reading more and contemplating more in order
to have more inner experiences?*

You have the love and protection of the Mahanta at all times. Not everyone has inner experiences or sees visual images during contemplation or in dreams. Some people develop a feeling of love and let it guide them around the usual obstacles. There are also those who get a touch of God's hand in some way and then are unable to find it ever again.

Please be patient, and let the ECK bring you what is good for you as you are ready. Having experiences with some of these manifestations of the Light and Sound of God before one is prepared does nobody any good. There is no advantage to wading in water over your head.

You have the love and protection of the Mahanta at all times.

FINANCIAL BALANCE

I am living with my brother and his wife in a very hostile situation. They make fun of me for doing spiritual exercises for hours. I would like to move out and get my own apartment, but I am not making enough money right now.

I appreciate your request for help. It is best to get one's physical and personal affairs in order first. Myself, I would use my income to get my physical life in order.

Divine Spirit began working on your request the moment you dropped your letter in the mailbox. But we must also do our part to straighten out personal affairs. As we put effort into bringing harmony and balance into our life, then these efforts are enhanced by the subtle, often direct, intervention of the ECK, the Holy Spirit.

Balance is the most important thing to achieve right now.

The Spiritual Exercises of ECK are meant to be

done no more than twenty to thirty minutes a day unless there is an experience underway that must be completed. Slow down on the spiritual exercises, and don't spend more time on them than is suggested above.

Can You Serve God Too Much?

Do what you feel inclined to do. The ECK takes each person through experiences when they're needed.

A friend on the path of ECK recently remarked that I wasn't attending meetings. This made me concerned about how to maintain a personal balance in my responsibilities and my spiritual life. I want to be true to myself.

To answer your question of whether to participate in local spiritual activities if it does not seem right: Do what you feel inclined to do. The ECK takes each person through experiences when they're needed.

But to follow your inner direction may take diplomacy and understanding. Explain to the others, if you even feel it is necessary, that the Mahanta has you working quietly in the background. And when your inner direction changes toward outer service again, you'll be in touch to help where possible.

Those on the path of ECK are at every level of life and must have the freedom to operate where they are suited to be.

Balance in Helping Others

I feel that my purpose in life has to do with helping others. But I am not clear as to how to do this or what exactly is my purpose for being here. Can you help?

Doing something to help others must be a personal decision. The path of ECK is one of harmony and balance. Personal duties and responsibilities are attended to first before we leave home, in a sense, to serve others.

The Spiritual Exercises of ECK are helpful initially to open ourselves to a greater flow from Divine Spirit. Yet with receiving more of Its Sound and Light comes the need to give of ourselves in some manner to others. This giving, or outflow, serves to balance us in our daily life. It is best to go slow when stepping on the path of ECK, whether we wish to serve or to study.

Much of the insight you asked for will come from the Inner Master, that inner part of myself. This will come either directly or simply through a knowingness of what to do the next day upon awakening.

Trust this guidance from the Mahanta as long as you see it to be positive. But take your time and go slowly.

It is best to go slow when stepping on the path of ECK, whether we wish to serve or to study.

The Way to See Truth

The path to God seems so slow at times. Why does it take so long for people like me to recognize truth?

Most people have a deep longing to hear truth, but it is doubtful that many of them would know it if it were to fall on the ground in front of them. Nevertheless, the search for it is on.

Life throws problems at us: Is this the true Master? Would the true teachings be done in this or that manner? The centuries turn as on a slow axle.

The wayward make their hesitant way back to the source of life when all the petty parts of them have been dissolved through the disappointments and sorrows of living. Then, and only then, is there enough consciousness embedded in the Soul body to see truth when it steps quietly before It.

Is there any meaning on earth except that the people on it must bump heads and make peace not with others, but with themselves?

HOW DO YOU STAY IN BALANCE?

Balance is often referred to as an important aspect in life. How does one get in balance—and stay there?

The balance of outer and inner spirituality is the spiritual goal in Eckankar.

Someone who lives mostly in the outer consciousness is out of balance. This is the social consciousness. Someone who thrives mostly in the inner consciousness is also out of balance, but in the opposite direction. This is the isolated saint.

The balance of outer and inner spirituality is the spiritual goal in Eckankar. Neither too much nor too little at any particular time. That is a determination made by each person. Neither I nor anyone else can dictate what that balance is at the moment.

Every so often someone on the path of ECK says to me, "Please tell me if I ever get out of balance."

Yet when that time comes, he cannot hear my guidance. He may try to follow it, but he is like a robot in his actions. So he continues to make more spiritual blunders. He simply does not understand why everything continues to go wrong even though he is following what he thinks the Master is saying.

The ECK usually takes care of balance by giving certain experiences that restore one's ability to hear spiritually.

How do you get in balance—and stay there?

Always love God—no matter what happens in

your outer life. Once you realize the spiritual lesson behind your imbalance, you will return naturally to the mainstream of the Holy Spirit, the Light and Sound of ECK.

Life is trying to teach us one thing: to see the ECK, the Holy Spirit, in the eyes of all we meet.

3

SPIRITUAL HELP IN DAILY LIFE

I am looking for a new home. Is it all right to turn over materialistic matters like this to the Holy Spirit? Should I expect Spirit to find a buyer for my old house? Am I being silly?

How does one use the help of Spirit in daily living? The first thing is to act as if receiving the longed-for goal is wholly dependent upon our own ingenuity.

Then we must be willing to surrender the matter completely to God or Divine Spirit. It may not work out according to our wishes, because Spirit may see a good reason down the road why it would be a step backward to let our plan reach its goal.

How does one use the help of Spirit in daily living?

WHAT WOULD I REALLY LIKE TO DO?

How does one use the all-knowingness of Divine Spirit to make a decision about a career move or a new job?

The way to work with Divine Spirit in our daily decisions is to consider quite honestly: What would

43

I really like to do? One must put aside thoughts of asceticism, thinking that God loves us more if we are poor. A business decision must be made using all input that's available. What's good for me, my family? It must allow one to grow.

Any decision is not without setbacks, for that's the nature of life. What sets the spiritual student apart is that he gives it his best effort and more, staying open to the subtle nudges of Divine Spirit through the Spiritual Exercises of ECK.

These decisions I am not able to make for you, but the ability to do so yourself is well within your grasp.

TAKING CARE OF YOURSELF

Why can't I get and keep a job? It's been a real problem for me. Please shed some spiritual light on what I am doing wrong.

Life is trying to teach us one thing: to see the ECK, the Holy Spirit, in the eyes of all we meet.

Millions of people hold jobs; there certainly is one out there for you too. The question is Where are you looking and what are your skills? Line up your potential with your previous training. Everything builds upon what we've done so far.

Life is trying to teach us one thing: to see the ECK, the Holy Spirit, in the eyes of all we meet. This means that those who have the enlightenment, or work themselves into it, have the ability to know that the Spirit of God is always with them. From then on they find peace and contentment and accept themselves without apology.

Try to straighten out your physical-world affairs first. The Mahanta has been trying to give you a direction that is for your own good. The message from this inner guide is given in quiet ways, through the words of your friends, in the heartfelt nudges that come to you in moments of silence.

Take one step at a time, little ones. The little ones will lead you to where you belong right now. There is too much straining and pushing, and this is responsible for shutting out the words you so need to hear now from the Inner Master.

Take one step at a time, little ones.

How much of an active role should one take as a spiritual student in taking care of daily affairs?

Too many on the spiritual path have a misconception that the ECK, the Holy Spirit, will do all good things for us if we just have faith, and also give a token nod to prayer or our daily spiritual exercises.

But under the surface, such people are actually passive and introverted individuals who never connect the need for material self-sufficiency with the path of ECK.

The individual is responsible for carrying his own weight in society in this lifetime. Earth is a training ground to learn the self-disciplines of Soul, which then lead It to a state of grace known as God-Realization.

Some will overreact to this direction and become full-fledged materialists. But there are lessons in that too.

Your Niche in Life

I am newly discharged from the Army, without a job. My marriage broke up recently, and my wife got everything. Can you help me figure out why my life's so bad?

First, you'll have to find a way to live. You need

information. Call the library, and ask for the reference librarian. In a sentence or two, explain that you're newly discharged from service and can't find a job. Rent is due at the end of the month, and you can't pay. Can the reference librarian think of someone you may call for temporary help?

The reference librarian may be able to get you the number of a public agency that helps people in trouble. Call the number the librarian gives you, and tell this person the same story. After a few phone calls, you should be able to find help to get you by.

Let's say that works and you find help for the moment—what about the real problem? You're a bright man, yet your life is a wreck. Have you ever sat down to figure out why? It's time to take an inventory of your life. Make a list of all the jobs you've held in the past twenty years, including the service, and give the reason you quit. One rule: Don't blame someone else for why the job washed out. Maybe it was somebody else's fault, but let's say the finger points at you. What did you do or not do in each job that caused you to move on? You've got to be honest with yourself in this personal inventory. Do the same with your marriages and relationships.

Be open to the ECK. There is a place for you, but you've got to have the love and humility to accept it.

About work: Have you applied at fast-food restaurants? Regular restaurants also need good kitchen help. Be open to the ECK. There is a place for you, but you've got to have the love and humility to accept it.

Another place to call for help is the Veterans Administration. They may have ideas or give you a referral to perhaps get food stamps. Public agencies are there to help people who need a boost.

Do the steps I've given you. In a month or so you should see what door Spirit has opened for you.

A MORE SPIRITUAL INDIVIDUAL

*How can I become a more spiritual individual?
I must struggle hard in my business to have enough
money to get married this year. As a result, I spend
most of the time thinking about making money, thereby
neglecting my spiritual needs.*

You are living the spiritual life when you conduct
yourself and your business in the name of Divine
Spirit. Each person who does this touches many Souls
during the course of the business day. Although he
may never say one word openly to his customers,
nevertheless the Spirit of God touches all whom he
meets, in some manner or another.

This life is for Soul to get the experience It needs
to open Its consciousness so that the Holy Spirit can
flow through It as a vehicle. A person lives the spiritual life when all his acts and deeds are done in the
name of Divine Spirit.

You are living the spiritual life when you conduct yourself and your business in the name of Divine Spirit.

PLANNING VERSUS SURRENDER

*How important are plans and planning? I wonder
about this in relation to adminstration of an office.
How does Eckankar handle planning and projects?*

As does most every organization, Eckankar operates administratively. Every time a problem comes
up, it is studied to see whether it is the result of not
having some essential administrative principle in
motion. Generally, that is the heart of a problem in
any office.

But the heart of our direction is in making plans
before using even an ounce of energy to carry out a
project. Plans developed by the gathering of perti-
nent information and reflecting upon it are the keys

to getting things done according to the will of Divine Spirit.

You know how to surrender to the ECK to handle your life. A person is obligated to do all he can for himself, but then, when his best efforts fail, he turns the whole bundle over to Divine Spirit to see how it can be done the right way.

Sharing Goals

Be sure of the people you would entrust with the dreams of your heart.

I have just finished school and am beginning to pursue a career. How can I know when to share my goals with others and when to stay silent?

Your basic question involves the Law of Silence. But in order to know when to speak and when to remain silent, you must apply the Law of Discrimination.

So the first question is who do you mean by others?

Be sure of the people you would entrust with the dreams of your heart. Heed the old saying: Never lend more than you can stand to lose.

A sad note about human nature is that the average person will try to discourage a dream that tries to reach beyond the ordinary. I call this attitude the great social leveler. It is afraid of excellence.

So if a goal is very important to you, keep quiet about it—or only share it with one or two close friends. Be sure they have given support to your past dreams and goals. Such encouragement can help.

Getting Things Done

It's amazing how little I am able to get accomplished lately. I have always been able to go through mountains of work, but now many little things inter-

rupt my day. Can you help me understand the reason for this?

You showed concern about how little work you set out to do in the morning actually got done by nightfall. More important details push your daily "to do" plans out the window. Don't be overly concerned.

Give your best effort each day, *and leave the rest to ECK, the Holy Spirit.*

Those outside of Eckankar will not believe it, but there is a tremendous resistance to the spiritual works of ECK. That resistance makes it an overwhelming job just to complete the simplest task.

When this happened to me, I put all my efforts behind the job highest on my priority list for that day. I did all possible to stay on track and complete it. *The principle: Do one job at a time, then hand-carry it to the next station.*

Of course, you can't always do that, but if you try to use this principle, you will begin to gain momentum over the resistance that has dug in against you. Once you gain momentum, things will go your way again for a while.

Concentration is the key.

Give your best effort each day, and leave the rest to ECK, the Holy Spirit.

INERTIA

I have a physical/spiritual affliction that the doctors are unable to diagnose. It's sort of a nervous disorder. All of the vitality within me seems to close off, suddenly, for no apparent reason. I am still able to walk around and ostensibly function, but with no animation whatever—a "dead man." I have had this condition for so long that I have developed techniques for survival. But I am always in fear that it will jump up out of nowhere and immobilize me.

The cause of the feeling of deadness you described came to me almost immediately: You are in a line of work you don't like.

Of course, the solution is not to drop out. As Soul, a spiritual being, you chose the conditions of this lifetime as a chance to grow out of the mental shell that you've put around yourself for protection from things that hurt or threaten.

You need to do two things urgently: do something you enjoy that's restful and quiet, and do something special for someone else every day.

Something else to consider is "light starvation." Some people with a finely tuned nervous system feel the lack of sunlight greatly during the winter. There are light products on the market that supplement light intake. Such a product can make a world of difference in restoring a feeling of goodwill.

You need to do two things urgently: do something you enjoy that's restful and quiet, and do something special for someone else every day.

SNOWBALL TECHNIQUE

I've read about the Snowball technique. In your mind's eye you roll all your problems into a big snowball, throw it into the ECK Stream, that spiritual force flowing from God, and watch your snowball dissolve. What is the purpose of this exercise?

The Snowball technique is for those times when you don't have conscious awareness of the Light and Sound of God. Use this technique when problems are a burden and you don't know how to get rid of them.

Such spiritual techniques are tried-and-true methods that Soul can use in Its spiritual development. When the work is routine and everything is running without problems, you may not think you need them. But when something goes wrong, the first thing you do is reach into your bag of tools.

You can't outgrow such spiritual exercises.

SELF-SUPPORTING

My husband has to retire because of his age, and we will receive a government pension. This is really bothering me because I have always believed that someone on a spiritual path must be self-supporting. I am not finding it easy to come to terms with this. Can you help?

In regard to your husband's retirement and having to accept a government pension: Accept it without guilt. You've been paying into the system, and now it is returning the money you put into it as a kind of savings for retirement.

That's how our life is today. It is in perfect agreement with the spiritual laws.

FINDING SUCCESS IN WORK

Since the seventies, my work record has been bad. There have been very few jobs and long gaps in between them. Although I have filled out over three hundred job applications in seven years, it is an exercise in futility. Out of the three hundred applications, I got two jobs. Can you help me understand this?

Does your job record tie in at all to your experiences in the Vietnam War? The war tore a lot of GIs up inside because they feel they could have won the war but were held back because of political factors. In the meantime, they were helpless to stop the deaths and mutilations of their buddies.

When something goes wrong, the first thing you do is reach into your bag of tools.

My brother was in the First Air Cavalry and got hit by a mortar. He came out of it OK, but quiet. People are now beginning to make studies of the impact of the war on GIs.

Maybe there's a VA hospital you can call; tell them your problem—that it's hard to hold a job. Do they have ideas to help you? Feel it out on the phone first—don't go in unless you feel that the people care.

ADJUSTING TO A NEW LIFE

In you is awakened the desire to return to God.

About four years ago I moved from my hometown to a foreign country. Newly wed, my heart full of love, I thought all obstacles would be leveled by time and love. I was wrong. I still cannot adapt to this new country and language, and I feel lonely. I need to find peace of mind and get rid of this feeling of being a bird without wings.

Often the Holy Spirit has reasons for putting us where we are until we've learned certain spiritual lessons. It is true that most of us feel more comfortable around our friends and loved ones. In a way, you are homesick. This experience is making you very much aware that you, as Soul, are also separated from your true spiritual home.

In you is awakened the desire to return to God. This spiritual side has a physical counterpart: your desire to someday return to your country. If that is the only way you feel you can ever be happy again, let Divine Spirit work out this problem for you. It may take time, for Spirit works in Its own way and in Its own time to bring relief to those who ask.

A way to let the ECK, or Holy Spirit, guide your life is to say inwardly (and often): "Thy will be done."

PRESENCE OF LOVE

I live in a war-torn country that is nevertheless making great strides forward toward an equality of races. How can I help this in a spiritual sense? I work as a nurse.

The world you describe is the kind of world that the spiritual student finds himself in: The unending play that swings back and forth between one kind of power structure and another. We do the best we can in sorting out our personal lives and making things better for others.

We don't do this out of a desire to improve the social conditions of society, but rather as an act of benevolence done out of love for God. This is the difference between the spiritual student and the social reformer.

Your presence is of utmost importance in your country during these potentially volatile times.

You are in the nursing profession and respect life in all forms, which is a good background for any spiritual student. There is never an absolute, perfect equality of any kind as long as Soul is in the lower worlds. This does not mean, however, that we stop working for whatever can be done to make it easier for the next person.

As the Living ECK Master, my function is primarily to find those Souls that are ready to return to the Divine Source.

BUSINESS ADVICE

I am considering opening a new business with a man I met. Can you tell me if this is a good idea?

As the Living ECK Master, my function is primarily to find those Souls that are ready to return to the Divine Source. As such, I am not able to give advice in personal business affairs.

May I suggest that you take your question to the inner worlds through the Spiritual Exercises of ECK? It is more important to learn how to work with the Inner Master than getting an answer through the mail.

As with any business matter, one must proceed with great caution. A talk with the banker you plan to get the loan from can give valuable information to make a sound decision. He will have seen your situation before, in one form or another. If possible, get two additional opinions from successful business-people you trust.

MANKIND'S PURPOSE

We live in northern Europe and were very conscious of the effects of the Chernobyl accident. How can we help with this? Can you give some perspective?

The spiritual need in Europe is far greater since the accident with the nuclear reactor. Not many people know the enormous capacity of the ECK, the Holy Spirit, to change the consciousness of man, but when mankind forgets its purpose for existence, a calamity occurs which reminds people that earth is only a temporary school.

Only that done in the name of God for spiritual unfoldment will mean anything at all when it's time to leave this temporary school. So keep your attention on the high and holy things of Divine Spirit.

SPIRITUAL OVERLAP

I have created a prosperity seminar which introduces people to some important spiritual principles. It is not linked to any particular path or teaching.

Is this a way people can be gently introduced to the golden wisdom of Divine Spirit?

There is a need for many to learn how to bring a more spiritual element into their lives. If they do not actually become more wealthy in material goods, at least they might reach such a goal spiritually.

Misplaced Trust

It would appear that everything I have touched has turned to ashes. My business has been one gigantic disappointment. I have boxes in my garage full of deals that never happened. After ten years of intensive effort, why has not one transaction been successful for me?

In time, I think you'll find yourself able to piece together an honest living for yourself again. Even though times are extremely hard now, you will look back upon them as the most spiritually productive in your whole life. This alone will give a sense of worth that no one will be able to take from you.

It may not seem so, but a divine chain of events does trace its way through the conditions of our lives. This is especially hard to understand in times of difficulty. As you've noted, misplaced trust has been your downfall. There is a way to love others and still be able to see behind their motives and act accordingly. I think your experience of late has taught you more about yourself and other people than you have learned in all the rest of your life.

Life, in some way, requires that we surrender to it all the things most dear to us—if we would have its secrets.

Your past loss has been a necessary loss, if only

Life, in some way, requires that we surrender to it all the things most dear to us— if we would have its secrets.

for you to realize why it is no longer necessary. Be aware, for the ECK is opening doors for your advantage.

MONEY AND SPIRITUALITY

I have feelings of guilt about my job. It is a good one, but I keep feeling I should quit. Is there anything wrong spiritually with earning money?

There is a misunderstanding about God's will for his children. God loves both those Souls that are rich and those that are poor, because God loves Soul. Soul is a divine spark of God.

God loves both those Souls that are rich and those that are poor, because God loves Soul. Soul is a divine spark of God.

It's all right to earn a respectable livelihood, if that's your wish. The ECK wants to bring the fullness of life to us, but we must set aside the fear and guilt that blocks our success.

There is usually somewhat of a struggle when we move into a higher state of awareness, and that is natural. The problems in life can be dreaded with fear, or they can be seen as opportunities for growth—and a challenge.

You must make up your own mind as to what you want to do. Consider all parts of your life, the financial and emotional included, and do what seems to be common sense. Then plan and work carefully.

LOOKING AT A PROBLEM

I have a damaged back muscle and work in a job that strains it every day. It's been there ever since my tour of duty in Vietnam. I quietly suffer until the time clock says I can stop causing pain to my body. Isn't there anything I can do in this physical world that won't hurt me so much? I am also having trouble remembering my dreams. What does this mean?

Let's start from the beginning—with the spiritual side. Some people don't remember their dreams because of fear that a nightmare will come instead. You've been in Vietnam. These things are being hidden for your own sake. When the heavy memories have finally dissolved from the emotional and mental bodies, then your dream memory will come back.

If you don't remember dreams, don't be too impatient, for you will when you are able to handle them. In the meantime, look for some help from Divine Spirit in daily things. Do you have any idea why you are having all this trouble?

Regarding work: Creation is finished. Therefore there is a way already established for you to make a living. Two of my friends here wash windows for businesses. They charge so much per window; they've found financial independence and security.

Have you seen doctors about your back? The first doctor doesn't always have the answer, and it looks as if the trip was not worth the trouble. But this visit helps narrow the search for the next doctor. We have to look into every source of healing that makes sense. The ECK, or Divine Spirit, is behind all healing.

To get help on earth, the surest way I've found is to go to doctors, go to personnel offices, and do everything I can. Life has been hard for me also at times, so much so that I know there is always the straw that can break the camel's back. But I also know from hard experience that there is always a way out.

If you don't remember dreams, don't be too impatient, for you will when you are able to handle them.

TIMES OF NEED

I've recently been informed that I will soon be out of a job. My career and future job possibilities here are ruined. I would be grateful to know what brought all this on.

The moment you drop your letter of request in the mailbox, the ECK begins to work to bring the spiritual upliftment that you need in times of trouble. Its first concern is that you have the purification needed to take you into the high spiritual planes.

Crises and troubles push us against the small self within us. The conflict between what we think our life should be and what the ECK has in store for us is quickly resolved in favor of the individual's spiritual growth.

The greater spiritual advances are made in times of extreme stress.

The greater spiritual advances are made in times of extreme stress. When there's no place else to go, true surrender of our cares and worries to the Mahanta occurs. The Holy Spirit provides a way out of the darkest, most threatening circumstances.

IMAGINING

I know that if I imagine what I want and see it inside myself as real, then those things will actually happen. But how do I balance what I want and still leave other people their freedom? Especially when my desires involve others?

Let's say a person wanted companionship. He might put the request to Divine Spirit, then do those things out here that he had to do to get ready—shave, dress nicely, whatever. Then he would leave the results to Spirit.

But if the person directs his request, saying, "That is the person I would like to share my life with," maybe his desire is not part of that other person's life scheme. He'll probably find what he imagines won't come true.

It gets into the freedom of another individual.

When you don't put a definite shape to what you imagine, Divine Spirit can have unlimited freedom to fill that mold. But if you put a limit to it, you often strike out because you've allowed for only one possible outcome.

Getting an Education

I am trying to decide about a future career and an outer goal that is right for me. I was wondering how important a college education is today. Will attaining all of that mental knowledge affect my spiritual unfoldment? Also, does God care what one does in regard to a career, or is that up to the individual? Is there some way I can tap into what God wants me to do?

How important is college today? It depends upon where you live and your cultural background. Pockets of golden opportunities dot the earth. Everything is of the ECK, of Divine Spirit. We live where we do because of what there is to learn there.

Allow yourself a lot of breathing room when picking a career. If you lock on to a certain profession too soon, you will miss many chances to grow spiritually. Yet in the meantime learn all you can, no matter where you live. Learn for the joy of it. If your goal is purely to get rich, you will box yourself into a dull life.

Times and conditions change for each generation. A secret I've found that always helped for promotion was to do as well as I could in everything. Success has a way of finding those who always do their best.

God just wants you to become a Co-worker. You can be that anytime and in any place.

When you don't put a definite shape to what you imagine, Divine Spirit can have unlimited freedom to fill that mold.

Standing Up

How can I be a spiritual student and still stand up for what I believe in, such as the abortion issue?

The abortion issue is an emotional one. If you believe in something, do what you can through community groups already established. This is how the spiritual student becomes a vehicle in a quiet way, standing behind issues that he feels strongly about, issues that threaten to rob him of basic freedoms of choice.

Then if you can find other ways to blend in a spiritual viewpoint, this gives added impetus. Let people do what is comfortable for them, because that is where their talents will shine. The fight to preserve our freedoms is unending and will change faces again and again. The ultimate purpose of the negative power is to enslave Soul in the clutches of the materialistic world. It is that simple.

Let people do what is comfortable for them, because that is where their talents will shine.

These are perhaps the most trying, yet most significant times ever encountered by people in their search for truth. In truth, the path of the Master is his own path. Although we can learn from his experiences, our unfoldment depends entirely upon our own encounters with the nitty-gritty of life.

Spiritual Protection

A friend committed suicide. People asked, "Where was his spiritual protection?" I didn't know what to say. Can you give me any insight on this?

A person always has free will. Even the Mahanta cannot give anyone protection unless that person allows him to do so, because that is the spiritual law.

In dealing with people who are out of balance, you

must remind yourself they are human beings who need love, compassion, and understanding now more than ever.

THE OPPORTUNITY OF THIS LIFE

A crisis at work brought up a question. I thought I did not care about death; if my time came, I felt I was ready. But now I realize I do have that fear, and during the recent incident at work, I could not face it in someone else.

ECK is an active path. We recognize that each experience that comes our way is spiritually instructive. If someone needs our help, we do what we can to the best of our ability.

A crisis such as you faced may be the Mahanta's way to kindle a new respect in you for the opportunity of this life. At the same time, the experience makes one dip into the well of reflection, to broaden compassion for an individual in trouble.

As you realized, fear of death has hidden itself in you. Now think about it: if there's room for fear of death, there is also room for its counterpart—a fear of living. On the path of ECK you will find that fear will diminish its hold on your life. There is the beginning of love.

Keep up with the Spiritual Exercises of ECK. They're your key to freedom.

On the path of ECK you will find that fear will diminish its hold on your life. There is the beginning of love.

IS EVERYTHING ALL RIGHT?

When I first began following the path of ECK, I had many spiritual experiences. In recent years I have not had as many. Is everything all right?

Many who first come to Eckankar lean toward the side of introspection. That's why they remember so many inner experiences. But these people often serve no useful spiritual purpose, since all their attention is upon themselves.

It apes an old attitude that's not useful today. Many feel that a person who spends his time soul-searching is more holy than a merchant who hawks his goods at the market. A highly spiritual person is actually one who has found the comfort zone that exists somewhere between the two extremes. People who first come to the path of ECK often have the habit of putting most of their attention on the inside. So it's natural for them to remember so many inner experiences, because they think that's what the spiritual life is all about. However, they've got it wrong.

Don't measure your spiritual unfoldment with a short ruler, because there is much more at stake here: spiritual freedom.

Their point of view is a simple illusion.

If they allow the Mahanta to help them grow spiritually, their hearts will begin to open. They will start to think of serving others first. The Mahanta is now bending the tree strongly away from self-interest toward compassion for others.

Though you may not recall many of your inner experiences, they are still going on anyway. In time, you will again remember more of your inner life. Don't measure your spiritual unfoldment with a short ruler, because there is much more at stake here: spiritual freedom.

The key to bringing divine love to us is to first give
selflessly of ourselves in some way.

4

DIVINE LOVE
AND HUMAN LOVE

*What is the difference between the love one has
for one's mate and the love Soul has for God?*

*Is one sort of love better than the other? And is
it still possible to fall in love with someone after you
reach God Consciousness?*

The highest love is a pure love for God.

A pure love for one's mate is the same as a pure
love for God. There is no difference. But, frankly,
pure love is a rarity—whether for God or for mate.

"Falling in love" usually means falling into karma.
Karma—good, bad, or neutral—sets the tone for a
relationship. For example, some couples love to fight.

The attraction between people of a high state of
consciousness is a mutual desire to serve God and
life. Such a couple join forces to help each other reach
even higher states of being.

A high, pure love is sweet indeed.

*The highest
love is a
pure love for
God.*

THE KEY TO LOVE

*I have been very lonely for many years, and I don't
understand how to bring love into my life. Can you
help me?*

We all experience loneliness at one time or another. But we each differ in the ability to adjust our attitudes to bring light and divine love into our lives.

Some make a great mistake in thinking that the way of ECK, Divine Spirit, is to withdraw from life. This is not so. It enhances our interests and activities, for we gain insights into ourselves through experiencing a wide assortment of activities, thoughts, and feelings.

The key to bringing divine love to us is to first give selflessly of ourselves in some way. It can be a small service for the ECK, although it can also be visiting the elderly or helping with some community project. But we must give of ourselves without any thought of reward.

First, do one small thing for the love of God, something small but important to us.

Loneliness is Soul's desire to find God. The Spiritual Exercises of ECK bring the Light and Sound of God.

The key to bringing divine love to us is to first give selflessly of ourselves in some way.

How can I learn the nature of love? I feel so afraid of it. Recently I had a dream where a monster was chasing me, and I shone a flashlight on it. I think the monster is fear.

Your question gets to the crux of the problem in spiritual growth: Fear is a poison that paralyzes a person, and the only remedy is love.

You've asked to learn the nature of love, and so it will be done in ways that are suited for you. Quite frankly, love scars the heart, but it is the only way to get purification.

You got a clear picture of the dream's meaning, that the monster is fear. The flashlight's beam is the blinding light of Soul that pierces the blackness of not understanding. A change can begin to come gradually into your life in regard to love, because you had the courage to face fear.

The heart of the ECK teachings is indeed love. For example, a businessman in his early forties got married recently, and the couple has a baby girl. All of a sudden he knows something about love and giving that had eluded him. A new world opened itself to him in a way that suited him.

A change can begin to come gradually into your life in regard to love, because you had the courage to face fear.

He'd seen parents and children every day, but until he had a child to care for and love, he was seeing in black and white. Please do not misread that I'm suggesting marriage. It is the power of love, however it comes, that makes you a new creature. And you will have it.

DECIDING IF LOVE IS REAL

How does one know if a relationship is based on love and is worth developing?

No one has the final word on love, but consider the following points in deciding if you really love someone: (1) Does he bring joy to your heart when you think of him? (2) Do you want to make him happy? (3) Will you love him for what he is and not try to change him? Will you let him be as he is and not what you want him to be? (4) Young people tend to fall in love with their ideal of love. This means that one has the ideal of a Prince Charming who is really a toad. Not all Prince Charmings are toads, and not all toads are Prince Charmings. (5) Don't forget your self-worth. How does he treat you—like a treasure or someone to be used?

Love is the expression of the ECK, Divine Spirit, on earth, and these points should give you a fairly good opportunity to see what kind of relationship you are in.

Common Sense

A male friend seemed to be a perfect match for me. Whenever we were together a tremendous flow of energy came through; he said being with me allowed him to travel to higher spiritual levels. Now as I look back I wonder if he was using me. I trusted him so much that I looked beyond his lies and unsanitary lifestyle, thinking it was a test for me. How can I judge situations like this in the future?

In matters of the heart, trust your common sense.

In matters of the heart, trust your common sense. Only you can decide whether any relationship is for your growth or not. I certainly do not endorse people who use the ECK teachings to get into bed with someone. Since that is a personal relationship between two consenting adults, it is outside the realm of my suggestions.

To give understanding in the future, the act of lovemaking does not raise anyone much beyond the astral, or emotional, level of consciousness, and certainly not to the high levels of heaven. Thus Eckankar will never become a sex cult.

A rule of thumb is that a person's state of consciousness can be perceived somewhat by his cleanliness. Every clean person is not necessarily a highly unfolded being, but it certainly is true that no spiritually evolved individual is habitually dirty or slovenly.

Do not fall for the trap of guilt or self-condemnation, but rely on the common sense you used in relationships before you started on the path of ECK.

No Strings Attached

How can one have a healthy, loving relationship without getting too attached?

Not to get attached is often taken to mean "not to get involved." It actually means not to let your idea of how things should be dictate the relationship. That kind of love has strings attached. It means always trying to have your partner do what you think is right.

Those with pure love do all they can to let their mates grow in every way.

So we come to the real meaning of detached love. It means to let others exist without forcing our will upon them. That is spiritual love.

Higher Levels of Giving

How can one remove ego when being a channel for Divine Spirit and give and receive without the little self becoming involved?

It's a battle that's never won as long as Soul lives in the physical world. We usually trip over ourselves when giving or receiving both human and divine love.

A friendship, for instance, may start on a high level. But once the two people begin to know each other better, the friendship is threatened when one gives a gift with strings attached. That's control, or power, trying to enter the relationship. See the ego at work?

Perhaps the hardest thing to learn is to offer a gift, but then to let the other freely accept it or not. This is nonattachment. Our training to be a Co-worker with God occurs in the classroom of our daily life. The lessons are tedious at times, but always thorough.

Those with pure love do all they can to let their mates grow in every way.

MIXED-RACES RELATIONSHIPS

I have heard that one should not get involved in relationships of mixed races. If true, why is that?

Everything depends upon the people, time, and place. If those three parts go against what a society accepts as normal, then members of that society will make life rough for the couple.

Let's draw a picture of an extreme case for you. Consider this: two people of the same sex *and* of mixed races who expect all the legal rights of a couple of opposite sexes. They would have a lot of problems in many parts of the world today. In a lesser way, a heterosexual couple of mixed races would have more problems in a lot of places than would a similar couple of the same race.

Weigh the odds, and do as you please. It all adds to your spiritual unfoldment if you love another.

It all adds to your spiritual unfoldment if you love another.

SANCTITY OF PERSONAL SPACE

A friend on the path of ECK who was visiting me disapproved of the nonspiritual books on my coffee table at home. Was I wrong in feeling he was getting into my personal space?

Whatever reading material we keep at home is our own business. The protection of our state of consciousness depends upon us. We must tell somebody else to leave us alone if they do not know better. There is a tactful way to remind a friend, who forgets, to give total beingness to others.

SURROUND YOURSELF WITH LOVE

How can I feel the love of God on the path of ECK when I am surrounded by people with negative at-

titudes? It seems so difficult.

It is difficult. There are two things you can do: (1) Be polite when these people are near you, but sing HU, the sacred name for God, silently. Listen to them while you sing, rather than getting into a long conversation with them. Say as little as possible while still remaining cordial. (2) In your imagination, see the Inner Master near you.

The negative force is using them as its channel to see whether you will agree with their opinions. Each confrontation is a spiritual test.

PROBLEMS IN MARRIAGE

My husband has told me that as long as we stay in the higher states of consciousness, our marital relationship will be smooth. But I can't always hold this high viewpoint, and he blames our difficulties on my inability to keep a spiritual outlook.

Generally speaking, marital difficulties stem mostly from these areas: (1) communication between the couple breaks down, (2) disagreement over finances (also communication), and (3) unfaithfulness.

The best way for any couple to address marital problems that have gone beyond their ability to handle is to seek marriage counseling. It's usually not any one person's fault that the marriage stumbles, although that is possible.

Those on the path of ECK must avail themselves of responsible counseling whether the problem is marital, health, or economic.

Those on the path of ECK must avail themselves of responsible counseling whether the problem is marital, health, or economic. That's the way to live in this world. Divine Spirit provides a number of different ways for people to choose the most appropriate solution. It is for the people involved to make their own decisions.

Communication Tools

Can you help me with any advice on how to keep the love flowing in my marriage? It's been strained lately.

Communication is a difficult thing to keep open in any marriage. One useful technique when things get strained is for one person to interview the other for twenty minutes, with notes.

The interviewer is free to ask whatever he wants. The only limitation is no question can be phrased so that it can be answered with a simple yes or no. That doesn't open communication.

The interviewer is not able to defend himself against any accusations but must sit there and take it. Of course, the roles change in twenty minutes.

The other spouse becomes the interviewer of hopes and dashed dreams. It is surprising what marriage partners learn about their companions that make them truly interesting people with goals too.

It is surprising what marriage partners learn about their companions that make them truly interesting people with goals too.

Soul Is Unique

Is there a difference between dating someone on the path of ECK and someone who is not?

The best answer is a question: Are two different Souls the same?

Naturally, not. What, then, do you look for in a date? Can you respect her beliefs and feelings? Does she respect yours? Are you a better, happier person in her company?

A light friendship is fairly easy to deal with, but when a special woman brings thoughts of marriage or a lasting relationship, look carefully at her family, her education, her plans for a family, her housekeeping habits, her handling of money. Are they like yours?

New love overlooks a lot of shortcomings, like a partner who spends more than she earns. But what happens when the debts pile up and a baby is suddenly on the way? Where is the money for doctor bills? Problems like these can make for two very unhappy people.

No matter how great your love for each other, things will always tug at its seams. The song of love is sung through respect and thoughtfulness for each other. They are the best assurance of a gracious and loving bond for years to come.

Dream Advice

I have been having recurring dreams which involve me, my boyfriend, and another woman. In all the dreams, my boyfriend treats me like extra baggage and ignores me while paying attention to her.

We have been having difficulties in our relationship, and for some reason, I don't trust him. How can I tell whether my dreams are intuitive or simply represent my insecurities?

A relationship without trust won't last.

A relationship without trust won't last. What is the source of this mistrust? Does he look at other women when you are out together in public?

Dreams can prepare you for a relationship that may be coming to an end. They will tell you something is wrong. If your partner is showing less affection toward you, you must decide whether to try to patch up the relationship or let it go.

Think of your dreams as advisers. They may point out problems and offer solutions, but consider all the facts before deciding on any important issue. Especially watch people's daily behavior toward you. Your dreams may suggest what behavior to look out for, but don't break up a relationship without some physical evidence to back up your suspicions.

No matter what happens with this relationship, try to be a greater channel for divine love. Love will overcome suspicion, which can destroy any relationship.

LOVING SELF

On the path to Self-Realization, how can Soul go about learning to love Itself?

Love others more. Then, loving yourself just happens.

LONELINESS

My wife and I separated a month ago, and I am feeling pangs of loneliness and sadness. We could not work out our differences. I would like to know if I can ever find someone I can love in a warm, caring way.

A marital separation is a painful experience. Both people in a relationship must approach the altar of love with gratitude, every day.

Our mate, above all, deserves the love that we can so easily show to others. Love means finding someone who can accept your outpouring of love.

Our mate, above all, deserves the love that we can so easily show to others. Love means finding someone who can accept your outpouring of love.

GOD'S PLAN

I am continually amazed at how hard life is for me. I am, frankly, questioning God's system—it seems too difficult. I have used all kinds of spiritual techniques, and I am still perplexed.

It centers on my personal relationships. I attract men who desire other women, even in the throes of the greatest love. No man seems to be able to love the way I am able to. What am I doing wrong to be so unhappy?

If everybody had the deep problems you have, I'd be forced to say, "Yes, God's plan for the unfoldment of Soul is impractical and unworkable." But very few people who write to me have the ongoing life of misery that you report.

By all accounts, you are an attractive, desirable individual. Yet in your personal relationships, you continually find yourself in the most unhappy circumstances. Let's see if we can shed light on the reasons for this.

As a personal study, have you ever put the names of all the important men in your life on a single piece of paper, with two categories under each: *attractions* and *final weak points?* In other words, what about each man attracted you to him. Be both honest and fair.

Then look at each of the men to see what it was about them in particular that caused a parting. There is a gap between what you think you're getting and what you finally end up with. You want to close the gap between illusion and reality *before* you invest too much heartache in the relationship.

I've known people with the uncanny ability to choose three alcoholic mates in a row. Maybe it wasn't so surprising since they looked for their companions in drinking establishments. Not one of these people realized they were always fishing in the same water, using the same bait. No wonder they kept coming up with the same kind of fish.

To turn around a life that's so often upside down,

There is a gap between what you think you're getting and what you finally end up with.

the individual must first make an honest inventory of all the factors that have caused the trouble. It's too easy to blame something outside of us for our troubles, especially if we do not like what we see in ourselves. But fixing the blame elsewhere will not make the trouble go away.

First make the list of all the men in your life, with their qualities of initial attraction for you. In that should be a clue why your relationships always end up wrong. Don't forget *where* you met them. What mutual interests drew you together? Did those same interests later rebound on you to destroy the very relationship they helped create?

Please be objective in your analysis of the men in your life. Otherwise you're no better off than when you started. You are a loving, giving individual. Now you must learn to find someone who is worthy of that love.

When you finish the list of the men, take another sheet and write "Arguments" at the top of it. Again, list the same men. Try to put down the thing you and each man mostly argued about. Besides outside relationships, were any of the arguments about money? List all of the subjects of disagreement with each man. That list should tell you something about yourself.

The answers you come up with on your list can help you see the next step in changing the conditions of your thought so that old patterns of the past can be broken and give you a fresh promise of a better future.

It's too easy to blame something outside of us for our troubles, especially if we do not like what we see in ourselves.

HELPING A FRIEND

A friend wrote me recently with her problems. I know we should not intercede for someone else, but I feel this is not so easy for me to handle alone. She asked me to write you on her behalf. How can I help her?

Write to her as planned, and do the best that's possible. It's interesting how she tells of asking the Mahanta's help, "but nothing has changed except for some improvements in my physical and mental condition."

When the ECK does help, the little bit is overlooked, which prevents any further changes from occurring.

Any healing that might occur is up to Divine Spirit.

You'll never pick up karma from a friend's misfortune as long as you conduct yourself with true love. This is a pure love that does not try to change conditions. This same love is called charity. It simply loves those it loves and is willing to leave it at that. Any healing that might occur is up to Divine Spirit.

ECK AND OTHER PATHS

Recently I have met and fallen in love with a devout Christian. He cannot follow my spiritual path, and in order to maintain a harmonious home I made the choice to become a Christian. But in letting go of my path and accepting Jesus, I feel such disloyalty and loss. How do I deal with these new feelings?

In regard to your personal situation, love will overcome all. This does not mean we will be without problems, but that love is holy and must come before any other consideration.

Follow whom you will in your heart. It is the same Holy Spirit working through yet another of Its instruments. There are many ways to reach the kingdom of heaven, otherwise why would there be so many religious paths, even within Christianity (Baptists, Episcopals, Pentecostals, etc.)?

Life does not bring two people together without a reason. Our past lives get mixed up in this, and we find new friends in this life are actually old acquaintances from before. Love is what drew you to your Christian friend. The relationship, if followed through, will bring spiritual enrichment to the person who recognizes the hand of Divine Spirit as the motivating factor.

One's inner life may be in harmony with whatever Master is able to be there in joy and sorrow. No one else, no matter how close they are to us, actually ever knows what all is in our hearts.

No one else, no matter how close they are to us, actually ever knows what all is in our hearts.

FACING FAMILY CRISIS

My wife and I are being torn apart by a decision. She wants to move to the Midwest to avoid an economic crisis here on the East Coast. I don't want to go, but I don't want to split our marriage. I even feel this problem could be caused by outside forces. Is there any way we can remain in our marriage and still have spiritual growth for each of us?

Fear is a destructive thing. Those who envy others who live a life of fulfillment will do all within their power to drive the wedge of fear between them.

There are always crises. To know this only requires a study of history. On the path of ECK, those who listen well to their inner guidance are often given warning by the Mahanta in advance of any problems to come which they can avoid.

There is no crisis of such scope that requires a move for your family to another state. If you want to move somewhere else, fine—but there is no local disaster in the making.

Others use warnings of fear in order to get control over a following of people, whom they wish to manipulate for their own uses. Notice—when fear enters, love departs. Those who love ECK will not let prophets of doom destroy their lives. The travesty would be in the destruction of a love bond.

Love the ECK, and all will be well with you.

How to Love

Fear has paralyzed me and left me cold and unfeeling. I want to learn how to love. Can you show me?

There is a lot of pain that goes with love, as you surely know firsthand. But the fire of love brings a change in spiritual outlook that cannot come by a shorter path. So, without love, we die; but with love, we are face-to-face with the agonies that burn the heart deeply.

On the one hand I see a person without love, who wants it. On the other hand, there are many who've had it, have lost it, and must decide whether to gamble on it again.

The secret is that one cannot live without love. You've got to find the kind that agrees with your spiritual makeup. Once you have it, you find it a delicate thing that can slip away like water through the fingers.

So, without love, we die; but with love, we are face-to-face with the agonies that burn the heart deeply.

How Do I Grieve?

It's been five months since my son was killed in an airplane accident. Although I have accepted his going and see him in my dreams often, I miss his physical presence. Tell me, how do I grieve?

The pain of losing a loved one is a sorrow common to all people, regardless of belief. It's natural to miss someone who has been so much a part of ourselves.

How does a person grieve? There's no one way

because our feelings about each loved one who leaves are different in each case.

To deal with the pain of separation, make an effort to help others. Offer to baby-sit someone else's children or pets. Or call the local hospital, and say you have a few weeks free in which you could be a volunteer.

Right now you have to go beyond your sorrow. Time heals all wounds, so be a volunteer for a while to give yourself time to heal. And write again, if you need to.

FEAR OF LOSING LOVE

When a relationship starts to spiral downward, I panic. I can't bear to see all the time and love I put into it be for nothing. Why do I experience this turmoil? Why can't I let go more easily?

The turmoil of lost affection that you are experiencing is actually Soul's desire for God.

The turmoil of lost affection that you are experiencing is actually Soul's desire for God. It makes you almost panic when a relationship goes other than what one could rightly expect from it. There is a lesson in all this, which is simply for us to trust the ECK, Divine Spirit, to bring to us the conditions that are for our best advantage.

I wonder if it's ever possible to get complete security in the lower worlds due to their impermanent nature. Every time we seem to have the world going our way, something comes up to upset our plans and leaves us in an emotional upheaval.

When a relationship with a dear one ends for whatever reason, the Holy Spirit already has something to replace it. The interval in which we wait is the difficult one, where our hearts cry out for understanding. When it doesn't come at the very instant of our need, we rush about in a blind fury, as if that will make things better.

Please remember that the Mahanta is always
with you, even in the darkest of times. We tend to
forget that, remembering his presence only when
things are on a steady keel. The Holy Spirit is already
working things out for you at this very moment, but
it's not possible to say that everything will remain
smooth for you from now on.

The nature of life is to face us with ourselves,
until we are able to handle the problems that knocked
us into the dirt yesterday. The higher you go into the
states of consciousness, the greater will become the
problems you encounter. This life on earth is a golden
opportunity for Soul to make important strides toward Its goal of self-mastery. Although the way may
be hard at times, know that the Mahanta is as near
to you as your heartbeat.

Your spiritual goals are in the right place, for you
strive to do the best in all things. A reminder is the
power of the spiritual exercises to give you a strong
aura that cannot be easily broken by outer events,
which will always try to pull you from the love of ECK.

I am always with you in all your concerns.

*The nature
of life is to
face us with
ourselves,
until we are
able to
handle the
problems
that knocked
us into the
dirt yester-
day.*

MISSING A LOVED ONE

*My precious husband passed away recently. We
were married for twenty years and loved each other
very much. It is unbearable to live without him. I need
your help.*

Your love for your husband and his for you shone
on his face for all who know what love is. Words of
condolence do not begin to put salve on the bite of
separation.

We love our dear ones deeply and miss them when

they leave us. But we know that the bond of love is greater than death.

He lives in your heart. When you are lonely and cry, look for him there, for he is happy to walk by the side of the Mahanta. He is now able to taste of the freedom he knew was there.

The sorrow of parting heals slowly. Let your tears fall, because they are tears of love too. And in your darkest hours, I am with you—giving all the love of God to you.

The sorrow of parting heals slowly. Let your tears fall, because they are tears of love too.

YOUR PERSONAL LIFE

I would like to know the implications of homosexuality from the spiritual viewpoint.

Thank you for your letter regarding homosexuality and living the spiritual life. Your personal life is for you to choose.

Divine Spirit begins uplifting Soul from Its present state into higher ones. As this happens, those practices which are obstacles on your next step to Self- and God-Realization will dissolve through the purification given by the ECK.

Whatever one does in his personal affairs is a matter solely between Divine Spirit and himself.

SOUL IS ETERNAL

Eleven years ago, our son committed suicide. This year our neighbor's boy did the same. What happens to those who do this? I just don't understand why he wanted to leave so badly.

We can only do so much when our dear ones shut out love and destroy themselves. Yet, take comfort: Soul is eternal.

You did all that was humanly possible to encourage him to anchor himself in this life. Please do not feel that you have failed him in any way. He knows you haven't and does not want you to carry an unnecessary burden of grief over time.

For a while, these unfortunate Souls wander in one of the inner worlds, the Astral Plane, lost. Some must relive their act of self-harm again and again. Thereby they learn how precious life is.

Eventually, the wheel of karma turns, and they are reborn. Their new life may be harsh, but it is to teach them love.

Your son's act of self-harm is of a temporary nature, for finally he, as Soul, will recognize his responsibility to life and serve it gladly without regrets. The Mahanta is working with him even now to help him adjust his spiritual viewpoint, so that he may become worthy of service to God.

I have been deeply depressed since a friend decided to kill himself. I think it was stupid. Ever since then, I haven't been able to contemplate or even hold a job!

Your friend's suicide was tragic, because he knew better. However, it did not end his spiritual existence but an all-important chapter in his life.

Why do people do acts that seem irrational to the rest of us? They are exercising their free will in light of their survival instincts. Many incarnations develop a fierce drive toward survival. But many, even those on spiritual paths, are only on the bottom rungs of this ladder of the survival factor.

There are many who have physical disabilities much worse than those your friend had. Yet these

Many incarnations develop a fierce drive toward survival.

people, some of whom are Vietnam vets, are cheerful, upbeat people. Why? It's a difference in how much more love they can show themselves. Your friend will learn to love himself more next time.

Remember—love is all!

WHERE IS LOVE?

I have many physical problems this lifetime and have had to overcome many obstacles. I've come to the conclusion that love is not for me this time around. How can I begin to have love in my life? Is it too late for me?

People can live together for years in a relationship and still not know love.

Your life certainly is an extraordinary one, and its uniqueness might let you think that love is only for others and not for you. You may find this hard to believe, but people can live together for years in a relationship and still not know love.

It would be wrong for me or anyone else to try to change your mind about anything that is between God and you, so I won't. This world has its torture camps (as in World-War-II Germany and elsewhere) and places for breaking the human spirit. Yet for some reason, a few among many who faced the same prospect of fear and death on a daily basis had a fierce desire to live. Why? Who can say? Perhaps the survivors were those with the strongest spiritual heartbeats.

Where is love? Again, who can say? We know it's all around us like an ocean, but where's the little stream to nourish the garden of our heart?

We don't mind if all the world has love, but we'd like a little too. Sure, we know about Helen Keller, who became blind, deaf, and mute at the age of nineteen months. With the help of Anne Sullivan, who was her friend and teacher, Helen became a renowned writer and lecturer. She raised funds for training the blind and other projects.

What I'm saying to you here is that people with exceptional problems like yourself must work many times harder than the average person for love or for anything else. But your success can also be much more than that of others.

Love begins in a small place in your heart. Love your music, which can reach out to bring love to others, and so the love in you can grow larger.

Love begins in a small place in your heart.

There are other people with handicaps who are looking for love as much as you. Some have found it. How? Can you connect with an organization of handicapped individuals to see how its members cope with their search for love?

Love is something we all need as much as air and light.

WHAT KEEPS ME FROM GOD'S LOVE?

How can I get closer to the love of God? I seem to stumble often.

First, one must learn to love, to give love to someone or something else. This means a sacrifice of one's self in the little things for the better interests of another.

First, one must learn to love, to give love to someone or something else.

The next part is one which few reach, because they cannot jump the hurdle of giving. This second step involves the art of receiving love from another. It takes humility to accept it with an open heart.

The third, unspoken part is when the love that is given or received is transformed and passed along to somebody else. No one can hold on to God's love and expect to get any more of it.

In summary, first one learns to give love; second, to receive it; third, whether it's given or received, the sender or recipient must pass it along.

It takes enormous courage to follow where love leads. Its fruits are bittersweet, most certainly. I doubt whether the love of God can really be known by someone who avoids human love.

Helping Children Grow Up

I raised my son alone, being both father and mother to him. Now he is married and has a family of his own. But he has always been a source of fear and concern to me, being very unstable mentally. I have found a man I like and would like to be with, but I am afraid of my son's reaction. Can you do a reading on him and find out why he is this way? Can you help me get over this fear?

It takes enormous courage to follow where love leads.

Spiritual law prevents me from getting into the background of your son without his permission. However, I can address your problem.

As you said several times, your fears are holding you back spiritually. They are keeping you from having a clear mind about what you would like to do for yourself. You've been both mother and father to your son, which was a noble but difficult task. The problem is that you've given so much of yourself to make him happy that you've neglected your own happiness.

See if your son can understand that you did everything possible to give him a good start in life. He is now healthy, has a good wife, and is the father of two children. He has the basics for happiness. Now that he's taken care of, you would also like to have a companion and happiness. Would he let you have that?

You can only do so much for someone else. You also have a right to be happy. There is no reason to feel guilty about that. Everyone has to grow up sometime, and your son can now do for his children what you tried to do for him. And you will always love him, but he cannot expect you to give up your whole life to him anymore. He's no longer a small, helpless child. Now he's an adult who must give his love and help to his growing family, as you once did.

You can only do so much for someone else. You also have a right to be happy.

We like to be with our own even after they've grown up and left home. But then the relationship between parent and offspring is that of two adults, no longer of adult and helpless child.

PASSING THROUGH GRIEF

I am presently going through a period of enormous grief over the death of my husband who passed away a few weeks ago. The extremely loving relationship we shared was rare and exquisite beyond description. I am hoping you can help me overcome some of the despair that I feel.

I've been carrying your letter with me for a week on a trip, trying to find words to fill the void left by the passing of your husband, whom you loved dearly. I find no words for a loss as deep as yours. The love you shared is a genuine and rare thing that will not be replaced.

If you are sincere in wanting to find a way through the awful despondency that has settled upon you, I can only suggest something that may turn your love for him so that others may share it through you. Love must have someone to go to, and the love you have for him must be given to another, one who needs it as much as you did.

This is your choice, of course, and you may find an alternate plan that suits your feelings better, but go to a retirement home and ask one of the people there to tell you what they learned about grief in their long life. Pick the person carefully. It should be an alert, sensitive individual whose face shines with goodness, kindness, and humor. Imagine that you are a child asking a teacher a difficult question, but that you are humble and want to know the answer.

I'm happy for you in the joy that lit your life, and I cry with you at your loss. I do send my love to you, with spiritual blessings.

Why do loved ones die and leave us here? My husband died suddenly, and I am bereft with grief.

Soul makes Its own decision about the worth of God's love for It.

Words alone cannot heal a broken heart. Only time can. Your husband went into the cave of purification by choice, because Soul makes Its own decision about the worth of God's love for It.

He knew that pain is a cleanser, but also that he could leave it behind by rising into a state of consciousness where it simply can't exist.

He's happy now. I'm sure you already know that. Let time and his love heal your wounds, for they surely will.

HUMAN LOVE, DIVINE LOVE

What is human love and what is divine love? How can I learn to live divine love?

You want to know the difference between love and divine love. Begin with love, and that grows into divine love. I know that's not the answer you look for, but the mind has nothing to do with love.

Begin with the love you have. Love gratefully. This love expands your heart into a greater vessel which can hold yet more love. On the outside, divine and emotional love may look the same, but divine love is joyful, thankful. It gives itself fully.

Let love be what it will. Don't let the mind tell you one is human and the other divine. Just love without expecting its return.

By watching nature, we learn the reality of aging. Everything gets older and eventually returns to the soil—everything except Soul.

5

HEALTH AND HEALING

I have tried everything to relieve myself of a deep depression. I feel I am drowning. Please help.

I received your request for help. You've asked God to give you vision and the light to see with. It will be done as you asked, but in His time. Again, it will be done, but in your time. This means, God's gifts are already yours, but only as soon as you can open yourself to accept them.

Well-being is physical, emotional, mental, and spiritual. If there is an absence of well-being, there is a deficiency in one or more of these four areas. Always start with the physical, because it's easiest to begin with what's closest.

Well-being is physical, emotional, mental, and spiritual.

If you have worries about your health, have a doctor give you a checkup. Also, review your eating and drinking habits. Alcohol, for instance, leaves one doped and depressed. Sweets, especially chocolate, can be just as bad for some people.

It is ironic that when we're depressed we want to eat something sweet, which can cause depression. A vicious cycle.

Loud Sound

I am having some health problems after enjoying a strong body for most of my life. The Sound of God, the divine Sound Current, is very loud. Am I going through a spiritual or physical change?

You mentioned a change of health and the increase of the Sound Current, that aspect of the Holy Spirit one can hear. The natural effect of a changing consciousness can show up as both physical and emotional. It requires us to adjust our habits of eating and perhaps even the spiritual exercises.

In my case, I've found that aging had an effect upon my feelings of well-being. It forced me to develop new dietary habits. I eventually gave up caffeine stimulants, such as are found in coffee, many soft drinks, and even chocolate. The stimulants, on top of my increasing spiritual awareness, made me too sensitive to the Sound of God.

We want the Sound in our lives, but too much of It can render us physically unable to carry on with our daily life. That means we must find a new balance. This means changing our habits.

Go about this rationally. Look at the foods you eat, for instance, then eliminate one food or drink that seems least useful to you spiritually. Continue to eat and drink your other foods and beverages. Watch for a few days if the removal of a certain food had any beneficial effect upon your feelings of well-being. If it did, don't use that food for several weeks. Later, you may wish to experiment: try to eat it again, but observe the effect it has upon your feelings of well-being.

Follow this plan with a second item of food or drink that seems *least* beneficial for your physical

The natural effect of a changing consciousness can show up as both physical and emotional.

or spiritual good. Go slow. You don't want to make massive changes to your diet. It could be too much of a shock to your body, and that would create unnecessary health conditions.

In effect, you're treating your body as a science lab. What you see there is unique: a reflection of your expanding state of consciousness. While making observations on your food and beverage habits, be sure to get any help you see necessary from experts in nutrition, etc.

We are a state of consciousness.

We *are* a state of consciousness. Everyone and everything in our personal and universal world has an effect upon us. We want to become aware of what these effects are. Then we can sort through them, nurturing the good ones and discarding the bad.

Too Far Open

My mother complains of an inner sound like people wailing or crying. She finds the sound distressing. Could you please give me a suitable explanation which I can pass on to her?

It's hard to explain some things to people who do not know the geography of the inner worlds, as many on the path of ECK do. She is hearing the cry of distressed Souls caught in a purgatory midway between heaven and earth. This means, between the Physical and Astral Planes.

People who are open to such inner sounds are often quite sympathetic to the suffering of others. They are likely to take in homeless animals and offer soft shoulders for the troubled to cry upon.

But their sympathetic nature actually works against them. They do not understand that people have caused their own troubles. This does not mean we should be cold about the sufferings of others, but it does point out that some people secretly like to injure themselves spiritually so they can complain to others about their problems.

Your mother is hearing the cry of lost Souls. These are generally people who died under stress or unresolved personal circumstances. Let her know God provides for their deliverance from purgatory (she is likely not to believe in purgatory) when they are ready to stop clinging to the sadness that keeps them there. They are in a temporary state, and angels will take them to heaven soon enough.

Then have her sing the name *Jesus*, if she is unwilling to use HU.

A final note: Faulty nutrition can also open up some people to psychic phenomena. Have your mother check with your family doctor to see that everything is in order in the health department of her life.

Divine Spirit often heals through the field of medicine and guides one to the doctor who is right for the condition.

YOUR RESPONSIBILITY

I have a severe allergy in my eyes which is very painful and affecting my eyesight. I have been to one doctor and am going to another, but the problem is still there. Can you help me?

The ECK began to work upon the conditions of your eyesight the moment you mailed your request for help. The ways of healing by Divine Spirit are truly endless. Often, the individual who has received relief does not connect it back to Spirit, but feels he has stumbled upon help by chance.

Divine Spirit often heals through the field of medicine and guides one to the doctor who is right for the condition.

The purpose of healing, however, transcends the

cure of a bodily condition. There is a spiritual reason that the illness occurred. The process of spiritual healing teaches us something about ourselves that we didn't know before. When the eyes are in trouble, we have to ask, What am I *not* seeing about my spiritual life that is causing me difficulty with my eyesight?

You see, the approach assumes responsibility for whatever is wrong. Once we're willing to shoulder the blame for our thoughts and actions, then the inner forces can begin to heal us, even as our understanding of the causes becomes known to us, perhaps through our dreams or other means of understanding.

Leave your problem in the care of the ECK, the Holy Spirit. Continue to look for a doctor to help you, and don't overlook a good nutritionist.

The process of spiritual healing teaches us something about ourselves that we didn't know before.

A Cure for Insomnia

Over the years, I've had a problem with insomnia that has gotten more severe. I have called on many specialists, but the insomnia is so all-prevailing that it is literally ruining my life. Can you point me in any direction?

I don't often like to bring up past lives, because people usually have enough resources at hand in their life to get a start on their health problem. With science so much in the forefront today, people tend to overlook influences from past lives because the idea seems hokey.

Nevertheless, perhaps a look into your past will give you an understanding of your inability to rest.

Today, some geologists poke fun at the notion of Atlantis, because none of their drilling into the ocean floor shows it to ever have been above water. Anyway, the civilization was very advanced in many ways that would make science today envious. But, as a whole, the people at that time were spiritually in what we'd call a state of infantile emotional development.

In short, they were efficient to a T, but the consciousness then had only the beginnings of what today we'd call compassion and humanity. Thus it became a common practice during the decline of Atlantis for doctors to perform euthanasia upon patients who were old, sickly, or malformed according to the standards of beauty in vogue then.

Somehow, you escaped notice of the authorities, even though you had a misshapen back, which left you in a constantly bent-over position. No one was too concerned about your appearance because you were a rural laborer, the equivalent of a migrant farmworker. Such labor was necessary because the maturing Atlantean society was much like ours today in that everybody was becoming too refined to dirty their hands at manual labor.

Of course, carried to its extreme, no society could exist for long under those conditions. Therefore, you and other members of the lowest class of laborers were not measured by the standards of beauty that applied to a growing segment of the population.

But you grew old and fell sick in the fields. This brought you to the attention of the medical people. It was determined that your useful life as a laborer was at an end. As with so many other unfortunates, a day and hour was set when you would be administered a drug that would put you into an eternal sleep.

The medical people treated you like an object

Atlantean society was much like ours today in that everybody was becoming too refined to dirty their hands at manual labor.

without feelings, speaking clinically—without grace—about the removal of your body and belongings the morning after. You were terrified of what amounted to a death sentence, and this fear is the reason for your fear of sleep. And while you've suffered from insomnia for a long time, it's gotten worse as you approach a condition of aging similar to the one in Atlantis. The aging is the trigger.

Soul cannot die. You did not know that in Atlantis. To bend this condition of fear back to a more reasonable place, I suggest you find a way to be an aide or a volunteer who works with small *children*. (Best of all would be to work with emotionally—not physically—handicapped children, so you can come to terms with the emotionally bankrupt Atlanteans who caused you so much trouble in the past.)

Soul cannot die. You did not know that in Atlantis.

You need to feel and see the continuity of life. Mainly, you must find a way to give your love to little ones. It must become unlocked and flow out into the world.

You now see yourself as the center of your world; you must make others the object of your love, which has to pour out from you. It may be hard to do this at first, so start small.

RELIABLE KNOWLEDGE

How reliable is the information we get from telepathy? Can it be affecting my health?

While it is true that telepathy is one method of communication between the mind and senses, it is also under the unstable psychic law. That means the knowledge will be reliable until you trust it. By that time the individual is certain that he's the reincarnation of Christ or some other departed Master.

Then society will put him under psychiatric care in order to be rid of his nuisance. That's life.

If you know anything at all about the workers of the negative field, you will see immediately that the Dark Force has tricked you and is playing with you. I sincerely suggest that you visit or call the United Way for referral to a licensed professional counselor (see the white pages of the phone book). See if they can direct you to someone who can give you insight into this problem.

CURING WINTER BLUES

I have been very sad lately but try to put on a happy face for others. Nothing seems to help. Recently I lost both my dog and cat, plus my husband's been down with the flu.

Winter causes some people to be depressed because of less sunlight.

It's easy to see why you'd feel down because of losing your dog and cat, and having your husband sick with the flu. Since your letter in January, you'll have seen changes in your situation.

Winter causes some people to be depressed because of less sunlight. So they try to balance that with eating more carbohydrates. Often they substitute soft drinks and other foods with a lot of sucrose, table sugar. Better would be complex carbohydrates like pasta, cereal, and potatoes, and other vegetables. There are also full-spectrum lightbulbs to give you more of the correct light.

Back to sugar a moment: If you feel depressed and take it in some food or drink (to feel sweetness), it'll actually make you more depressed shortly. Diet can play a major role in how we feel. Chocolate can cause severe depression in some people and should be avoided if that's the case with you.

Since you wish to make an effort to find the reasons, consider getting a checkup from a competent physician to insure your health is as it should be. Private counseling may be more difficult to come by, but if it's available and affordable, consider the option.

LONGEVITY

How can we live longer? I have been studying the use of herbs as stabilizers of well-being.

By watching nature, we learn the reality of aging. Everything gets older and eventually returns to the soil—everything except Soul.

There are many ways to improve our nutrition and have a long, happy life. Don't overlook the offerings of science. It has increased the average life span in many countries from forty and fifty years to better than sixty and seventy years.

Everything gets older and eventually returns to the soil— everything except Soul.

ROOTS OF A COUGH

I have an awful cough that began after my wife passed on. It is embarrassing to be at meetings; I have to leave until I stop coughing. I have seen four different doctors without getting help. I am asking for spiritual assistance and would appreciate your help very soon.

You have done the correct thing by seeking help from four different M.D.'s, even though none was able to help you with your problem. I am not a licensed physician and so cannot pretend to offer a cure where they have failed.

It is interesting that this problem began *after*

your wife passed on. While it is possible that you con-
tracted something in the hospital during your four-
month stay, it is also possible that since your wife
translated from this physical life, your diet has
changed for the worse. This may or may not be the
case: you are the best judge of that.

In my own experience, I have found certain classes
of food cause phlegm in my body. This does not mean
that another person will have the same sensitivities.
Any kind of a dairy product causes mucus: cheese,
yogurt, cottage cheese, or milk. Bread and crackers
do the same thing. It even got so that fruit caused
phlegm.

A body needs protein. I avoid beef and pork
(except for bacon on occasion), but I do eat chicken,
turkey, and fish—broiled or baked, never fried. Baked
red potatoes seem to sit better than brown potatoes,
although I do eat mashed potatoes with a homemade
sauce of fresh garlic, sunflower oil, and water shaken
in a jar or a blender.

Flours (the bread, crackers, and gravies) also
cause congestion. But I'm able to eat salad—except
no iceberg (head) lettuce—and hot and cold vegetables. In addition, a nutritionist might recommend
a balanced vitamin-supplement program.

This is only my control diet, when regular eating
has given me too much congestion. (It may not be
good to someone else.) Otherwise, I eat many of the
things I used to.

DANGERS OF THE KUNDALINI

*Years ago, I was initiated by another master, and
after much meditation, the kundalini power was
awakened. My health has deteriorated ever since.
Why? Can you help?*

The kundalini is a powerful force that is better left asleep. Once it starts to move up the spinal column, there must be some place for it to go—or like a flooding river blocked from its usual course to the sea by a landslide, the water overruns the banks and causes great damage to the farmland on either side.

Meditation is a passive discipline that shows a disciple how to see the Light of God, but then what? It's like the pilot who knows how to take off but never bothered to learn how to land the plane! There must be a way to return this love or it will burn and damage the inner and outer bodies. This is why I suggest the spiritual exercises or contemplations be kept to no more than twenty or thirty minutes a day. The rest of the day is for one's job, family, and recreation time.

Meditation is a passive discipline that shows a disciple how to see the Light of God, but then what?

Now, what to do? The Law of Karma is exact in its measure. To cure a health problem several years in the making often takes a like amount of time for healing. There is no magic way to get an instant, long-term cure without our taking a part in the rebuilding.

Find a good doctor who knows nutrition; an expert in this field can help you back on the road to recovery. Be assured that the Mahanta is always with you to steer you to people who can help you to better health and the happiness that comes with it.

WRONG ADVICE

I have been having blood-pressure problems. The doctor has given me a prescription for the condition. A friend advised me not to take the medicine, and I'd prefer not to. What should I do?

Please listen to your doctor, and take the pills he

wants you to take for your blood-pressure problems. If you are not sure about his diagnosis, get the opinion of another doctor. Don't take the advice of a friend who says to ignore the doctor's prescription.

You want to get good medical advice from a doctor for health problems, not an uninformed opinion from a layperson, even if it is a good friend. The ECK, the Holy Spirit, also heals through physicians, dentists, and other kinds of doctors.

The ECK, the Holy Spirit, also heals through physicians, dentists, and other kinds of doctors.

AIDS QUESTION

What is the truth about the phenomenon of AIDS, and how can we protect ourselves from it?

AIDS is just another of the serious illnesses that periodically sweep the earth.

In the fourteenth century, for example, the Black Death, or bubonic plague, killed from a quarter to a third of Europe's population in three years. Standards of hygiene were much lower then than today. Bubonic plague was transmitted by the fleas on black rats. The waste of its victims gave others pneumonic plague. Europe had no defense against either, because of its low consciousness about hygiene.

The problem with AIDS again is a matter of awareness. Health agencies have made available much information of how to be careful with sexual intimacy. It means taking the trouble to first find out the state of your partner's health and other considerations.

WAVE FROM THE PAST

Some extraordinary fear and pain has been activated by my recent motherhood. I am at the bottom, feeling trapped. Can you please take me to a healing place in my Soul body and wash me of this agony? Perhaps give me an understanding of its source.

The fear and pain which have resulted after your recent motherhood is due to both outer and inner conditions. In a recent life in New England you gave birth to an illegitimate son. The late 1600s were not very understanding times for a girl in your condition.

The childbirth in this life triggered a recall of that life, and the old feelings of shame and abandonment that made you want to end it all. To your credit, you raised the child and learned the spiritual lessons that accrued from that experience.

I would encourage you to follow up with counseling by a professional. Also have a nutritionist make sure that the demands of motherhood are not outpacing your normal level of nourishment.

SPIRITUAL BOOSTS

Why do some of us have to live with chronic disease in this life? I am an epileptic.

It has been difficult for you to cope with epilepsy for most of your life, but it is exactly that which gave you the spiritual boost to find the teachings of ECK. In this case, your burden proved to be your ladder into the higher states of consciousness.

In this case, your burden proved to be your ladder into the higher states of consciousness.

KARMALESS HEALING

How do healers stay free of karma? What is karmaless healing?

The safe way to handle requests for healing is to turn the person with the request over to the Holy

Spirit. On the path of ECK, you will perform the karmaless action if you instruct them to write to me so that the healing may be accomplished through Divine Spirit if It so wills.

Spirit acts in a way that is for the good of the whole, sometimes bringing a healing of the emotions or the mind instead of the body, because that is in the best interests of that particular Soul's unfoldment.

For one to put himself in the healer's shoes is to unknowingly accept the karma of the person who requests the healing. At some time in the future, the karma must come due if it is not passed off into the ECK, the Holy Spirit.

MORE THAN BAND-AIDS

I'd like a greater understanding of the difference between psychic healers and other kinds of healers.

At some time in the future, the karma must come due if it is not passed off into the ECK, the Holy Spirit.

Regular healers help fix problems people cause themselves by putting a Band-Aid on them. If you go to a doctor for a cut, he cleans it and applies a bandage until it can heal naturally. He does not try to tamper with a spiritual condition he is not quali-fied to heal, which psychic healers often try to do and thereby set up more causes to be worked out as more problems.

A difference between psychic healing and spiri-tual healing is that psychic healing leaves you in the same state of consciousness, perhaps temporarily alleviating symptoms caused by an attitude you hold. However, spiritual healing helps change the attitude which caused the problem, so it can go away and not recur.

The problem surrounding healing is karmic. The ill person once broke a divine principle through ignorance. Psychic healers can ease the symptoms for a while, but eventually the sickness surfaces again with a new face.

In the meantime, the healer is accruing the karma from all the people he heals with the psychic force. Someday the debt comes due. There is more to healing than erasing the outer symptoms for a few months or years, or until the passion of the mind that lies behind the illness produces the next symptom of arthritis or cancer.

When the Living ECK Master is asked to help, he puts the entire matter into the hands of the ECK. It, in Its divine wisdom, sees whether or not the individual has learned to control the mental aberration that made him ill. If not, there is no healing. After all, Divine Spirit wants only the education of Soul so It can be a Co-worker with God.

Divine Spirit wants only the education of Soul so It can be a Co-worker with God.

SEARCHING FOR HEALTH

I am plagued by rheumatoid arthritis and don't know where to turn next. Can you give me any direction toward healing this problem?

By now you've probably seen a lot of doctors about it. There is always somebody on earth who knows more about a certain condition than anybody else.

If you haven't already, try to find a homeopathic chiropractor who has some knowledge of nutrition: the effects of foods on the body. For instance, nuts and seeds (raw and roasted) are not good at all for some people, while others thrive on them.

This isn't much of a lead, but your search for health will be guided by the inner principle that I am, the Mahanta. Divine Spirit acts in Its own way and in Its own time to bring about what is for the good of all.

At times Divine Spirit heals directly, at other times It leads one to the right medical doctor. Sometimes It will assist in the healing and treatment we are presently undergoing. On the one hand we must inwardly turn everything over to the guidance of this Supreme Force while making every effort to find the most suitable medical help.

SPIRITUAL FASTING

Can you give me some idea how enlightenment comes into Soul and heals the inner bodies, and what techniques help this?

Enlightenment is a gentle thing if it's right, if you're ready for it.

Enlightenment is a gentle thing if it's right, if you're ready for it. It gives you a different viewpoint, a different state of consciousness.

This also occurs when we do a spiritual fast and keep our thoughts on God, the Mahanta, or something spiritual. You'll notice that when you are on a spiritual fast, you treat people differently at work and at home. You're in a different state of awareness that day. You're pulled out of the routine or rut that the mind likes.

This actually works off karma. The hold of the material world, the attachments, are not as strong on you. This gives you a little more freedom of choice. It puts you in charge of your own life in subtle ways. Other people can feel this.

Most of our problems are self-made.

Sometimes there is something going on at work, something that's not too smooth for you. You can do a spiritual fast for a couple of days. You'll find that your attitude and your very words are different. You're not creating karma the way you were before.

Most of our problems are self-made. When things go wrong, if we take responsibility and do something that gives us greater understanding, life becomes easier.

This is how it should be, rather than having someone always giving us spiritual, emotional, or physical healings.

ACTION BY DIVINE SPIRIT

How do you solve a matter of healing when someone writes you with a request?

The problem is turned over to Divine Spirit which goes to work immediately, even before your letter reaches its destination. I do nothing of myself, but it is my responsibility and spiritual duty to act as an instrument for the spiritual power to flow out to all and help anyone who makes a request.

I cannot tell if a person's request will be fulfilled as he desires. Spirit will use Its own divine wisdom to help each one for his individual welfare. It may guide him to the proper medical doctor or in some other way address Itself to the condition behind the problem.

If the person will surrender all of the problem to the Mahanta, the Inner Master, the problem will be taken care of in due time.

If the person will surrender all of the problem to the Mahanta, the Inner Master, the problem will be taken care of in due time.

BREAKING FREE

I am at a crossroads spiritually. And I feel stuck. Is it possible to be a member of a spiritual organization without surrendering to a master? I have blocked myself inside for fear of spiritual traps which abound in different paths—I've encountered quite a few myself. A few years ago I abandoned all gurus and took to Mother Earth and gardening.

You've gone through some hard times, trying to

understand what part those past experiences played
in your spiritual growth. Some people have a very
delicate inner mainspring, like that of a watch. They
are hurt more easily by things which another might
take more in stride.

Inwardly, you saw the need to heal yourself.
That's why you took up tai chi and gardening. We
all need to feel in touch with something stable, and
you did too. But now that you've healed to a certain
degree, the inner nudge from the spiritual side is
again offering you a chance to grow. The idea is not
to hide from life: It is to live life, but without making
the same mistakes we did before.

The question you're now asking is whether you
need to join an organization (like Eckankar or something else) to grow spiritually. No, you do not. But
don't be a hermit either. People need people. That's
how things are. Join recreation groups or study
groups, even take classes—if that's what you want.
But be with people when you need to.

Some people do not fit within an organization
like Eckankar, and I respect that. You've come a long
way in healing yourself, but try to understand that
earth is not a rose garden. We all get hurt and cry,
but then we must get up tomorrow morning for those
who depend on us.

The idea is not to hide from life: It is to live life, but without making the same mistakes we did before.

THE PACE OF HEALING

I have asked repeatedly for healings from my terrible cancer. Please help me understand why I am still afflicted with it.

It is not I that do the healing, but the Holy Spirit,
which we call the ECK—if It sees any to be done.
You stare at the negative side of your life as if nobody

else in the world has any troubles.

Do you recall the story of the distraught mother who lost her child and came to the Master beside herself with grief? He said, yes, he would help her if she would but go door-to-door and find one household that had never been touched by sorrow or death. After spending a great length of time in doing this, she returned to the Master a much wiser woman. It became clear to her that the things in our life are not our own, merely things that are lent to us by the Spirit of Life for our growth.

You have a wonderful husband who loves you dearly. There is not anything more precious in this world than love—not health, youth, or beauty. If your ill health were ripped away from you in one day, there would no longer be the tie between you that you have today. And it is a good one in that both of you are able to give your love to each other if you so choose.

The Mahanta wants to show us how to make our life a bearable one by the application of the rules of common sense, which are those of the ECK.

The Mahanta wants to show us how to make our life a bearable one by the application of the rules of common sense, which are those of the ECK.

When calls for help come to me from victims of cancer, but the Law of Karma says that this is the best way for them to get purification of the mind so that they can get liberation of Soul, then that is the will of the ECK. I cannot interfere. There is help for you, but you must really stop and listen to the help that is coming to you.

SPIRITUAL TANGLE

I'm having scary visions. I have talked to a friend, who explained to me about the psychic I've been going to. He also said you may be able to tell me why I'm having these frightening visions.

The cause of the disturbing visions is mixing the psychic field with the spiritual way of ECK. A terrible storm develops within the human consciousness.

The safest thing to do is, first, get the psychic centers in your body closed. Call the United Way (see the telephone white pages in larger cities) or your local counseling referral service and ask for advice for your problem of scary visions.

See what counseling is available to you and the cost. If you take the step to seek qualified counseling, then Divine Spirit will begin straightening out your spiritual tangle.

GIFTS FROM GOD

I need your help on a problem that is devastating to me. Both my sons have been diagnosed with cystic fibrosis, a life-threatening disease. The doctor says they will live only to their twenties or thirties. My heart breaks daily over this, since they are truly beings of light. Can you give me some insight into why they chose this or what I did to cause it?

Our children are a gift from God.

Science is making new discoveries all the time about the cure of diseases. The Holy Spirit, or ECK, works in many ways to bring healing, even through the wonders of science. The doctors give your children a number of years in which science may find a way to help them. As a parent, I know that your children are as dear to you as your own life.

While the doctors and scientists are racing to find a cure for cystic fibrosis, ask Divine Spirit to show you the reason for their illness. What can you learn spiritually from it that cannot be learned another way?

Our children are a gift from God. Though we do

not own them, we do love them with all our heart. Until the doctors find a cure, be thankful for every moment you have with them, but remember to let your sons breathe and grow into their own dreams.

My thoughts and love are with you in these troubling times. I'm turning your problem over to the ECK to handle as It will.

HEALING FROM INNER ATTACKS

How can I heal myself from psychic attack?

Psychic attacks can be severe and can actually produce real illness. If this happens, get a diagnosis (if it is a safe procedure) from the medical profession or from an alternate branch of healing, to track the progress or deterioration of health.

Soul is eternal, without beginning or ending.

The ECK will lead one through a labyrinth of specialists (it seems endless at times) until the right combination comes face up and help is given to relieve the ailment. The long process of discovery is one of a continual broadening of understanding about the causes of illness.

Soul is eternal, without beginning or ending. It comes again and again to get every experience so It can become a citizen of the high worlds of God while still alive here on earth.

Divine Spirit works in many ways to bring about healing, if that is what It chooses to do. It may lead you to a doctor who is very good at healing your illness. Or you could be led to the right herb or herbalist.

PATH TOWARD HEALING

My son is recovering from a long illness. Can you help ease his pain? Would it help if I did the spiritual exercises twice or more a day?

Your request for your son's health has been turned over to Divine Spirit. It works in Its own way and in Its own time. How It will handle this, I cannot tell, for I am only Its vehicle.

It may guide you to the proper medical doctor or in some other way address Itself to this condition. All healing comes from the ECK no matter what vehicle It uses. Medical doctors and psychologists are legitimate healing agents on the physical plane. Once we seek professional help, then Divine Spirit will guide us from one doctor to another until the proper help is given. This is how the ECK often works, although there are the rare instances of miraculous healings.

Take your time with the Spiritual Exercises of ECK, for it takes each person time to build spiritual stamina.

Take your time with the Spiritual Exercises of ECK, for it takes each person time to build spiritual stamina. It's often helpful to keep a dream notebook, if your inclinations run that way. The path of ECK enhances our life, to guide us along our own path to God. With that I can help you as the Inner Master.

In time the curtain is drawn back, and we see the purpose of hardships that we have had to endure. There is a reason for everything that happens in our life, even though the greater picture may be withheld from our spiritual eyesight for the present.

Take each step in your physical life as it comes, with the assurance that the way has already been prepared by the Mahanta. It will be resolved in the best way for all concerned.

At their marriage, one couple made a "first cause" state-ment to each other. They each made a vow to help the other become a Master in this lifetime.

6
FAMILY RELATIONSHIPS

What does the marriage bond signify spiritually?

The marriage bond can only be sacred if it is sacred to the two individuals who have agreed to this union. If they are one in heart, how can they be divided? At their marriage, one couple made a "first cause" statement to each other. They each made a vow to help the other become a Master in this lifetime. They would help each other in conscious spiritual evolution, out of love, to reach the heights of God.

A true marriage has commitment by each person. Both realize the responsibility of that commitment. A marriage of the heart lets each of the couple remain an individual, but the two are as one.

> *A marriage of the heart lets each of the couple remain an individual, but the two are as one.*

FINDING TRUE LOVE

My husband isn't a member of Eckankar, but he evidently learned a great deal about contemplation early in life. Our beliefs seem different, but they aren't really. He isn't well physically, and we both know his time is short. I want to know if he is all right not being on the same spiritual path as me.

Life indeed leads us down unexpected but interesting trails. One such trail was the one that brought you and your husband together. The joy of a spiritual bond such as yours will continue beyond this life.

Your life with your husband has shown so clearly that not all students of ECK are in Eckankar. In fact, it's not even possible, in fairness, to create such categories of consciousness. Either one knows the Spirit of Love or he doesn't.

The same rule applies to members of Eckankar. Those who have the love of God within them belong to a spiritual race of advanced beings. Outwardly they may look no different from their neighbors, but they are carriers of the Light and Sound of God— even though not always conscious of it.

Either one knows the Spirit of Love or he doesn't.

RESPONSIBILITIES TO YOUR FAMILY

I am Japanese, and my husband is an American. My husband has been reading books about how the world is going to end in 1999. He wants to go to a community in Arkansas and grow crops. This would mean leaving me and our baby son in Japan, but he doesn't seem to care. Do you encourage people to leave their family if they want to?

For centuries people have predicted the end of the world. Needless to say, they've been wrong. The same doubts troubled people in the years shortly before A.D. 1000 as trouble others as we approach A.D. 2000. Such a prediction is not part of the ECK teachings.

The world will continue for many thousand more years. Therefore, there is no need for your husband to run off to another part of the world "to do good."

In ECK we know that our responsibility is first toward ourselves and our families. How can anyone expect to help others if he abandons his own family?

In any group, you will find people who are highly responsible as well as those who are not. Those who are not responsible to their own cause them much needless sorrow.

I find myself still aspiring to physical things, for example, the construction of my home. This has confused me. On one hand I am afraid that this is a negative attachment to material things; while at the same time, I feel I am merely fulfilling my responsibilities to my family.

I am grateful for your letter. Please know that one must provide for his family as well as possible. That has nothing to do with attachment.

God loves Soul rich or poor. God does not necessarily love the poor more. God loves Soul. Thus we can enjoy the things of this life and support our family with material goods with no feelings of guilt.

The path of ECK is merely to open our consciousness so that we can become greater vehicles for Divine Spirit. Thus ECK enhances our life and gives insight, strength, and understanding where we found only darkness before.

STAYING FREE THROUGH CHARITY

Does sympathy for a friend cause a transfer of karma?

You'll never pick up karma from a friend's misfortune as long as you conduct yourself with true

The path of ECK is merely to open our consciousness so that we can become greater vehicles for Divine Spirit.

love. This is a pure love that does not try to change conditions. This same love is called charity. It simply loves those whom it loves and is willing to leave it at that. Any healing that might occur is up to the ECK, the Holy Spirit.

TWO PATHS, ONE MARRIAGE

When I first became a member of Eckankar, my husband was quite agreeable. But after learning more about it, he is very much against it. I am not permitted to do my spiritual exercises or attend classes. I have been suffering severe illnesses and am in need of your advice.

Concerning situations where the ECK teachings bring a reaction in the home, it is better to step back from the outer works and continue quietly by yourself until matters improve.

You will continue to receive the love and protection of Divine Spirit in spiritual matters as long as you want them. I would rather see harmony in the home than have a family torn apart by differences of belief.

Much of the illness is due to the disharmonies that swirl about you, the fears and anxieties. For this I suggest the continued help of the medical profession, for Spirit frequently uses that means to bring physical relief.

Harmony in a family is a sacred thing.

Divine Spirit tends to hold families together whenever possible. I do not want a husband and wife to fight over their different religious beliefs. Harmony in a family is a sacred thing.

Members of my husband's family have been very

upset with us since we joined Eckankar. I have felt awful. I have tried contemplation, but only thoughts of anger come to mind. I've gotten some therapy to overcome these low moods. What can I do to help myself and my family through this?

It is good you are getting professional help to overcome the negative feelings that are affecting your family.

To help with your therapy, consider stepping back from the outer works of Eckankar until you can turn the corner with the personal concerns that are overwhelming you. The crosscurrents are too strong right now between your personal problems and trying to be active with the outer ECK works. This is up to you of course. You still have the love and protection of the Mahanta.

The turmoil in your family is a difficult time for all of you. It seems as though the lines are drawn as sharply as they were in the Civil War, when brother turned against brother for an ideal. All of it is needed for your spiritual enrichment, odd as that might seem from your vantage point in the midst of the hurricane.

At first glance, it seems an unfortunate thing to be in such difficulty, but the ECK always has some purpose, even in the most extreme situations. It is not the hard knocks in our lives that are of any real importance, but what we do when they hit us. The attitude is the measure.

It is not the hard knocks in our lives that are of any real importance, but what we do when they hit us. The attitude is the measure.

I had a divorce that I am unhappy about. I have four children; two live with their dad. This situation makes me very unhappy. Do you think it is too late to somehow gather all my family back together?

You might start by taking soundings of how each person you wish to be with again feels about it. A lot of pain occurs on all sides in a marital separation, and it doesn't go away overnight. Besides, as time passes, each of your family has gotten older and has begun to fashion a new life for themselves.

Parents who stay together in their marriage see the growing independence of their children on a day-to-day basis. But in a separation, the parents whose children live away may not be able to keep up emotionally with the growing independence of their children.

Growth and change are natural parts of living.

Growth and change are natural parts of living. We are unhappy when, for some reason, we cannot keep up with them.

So, you must look first at yourself with complete honesty. Do this by taking a sharp look at all the people in your dreams of a family as of old. Look at each person honestly. How old were they when they left? How old are they now? What interests did they have then? Now? The hard part, if there is to be one, is the condition of how things are *now*.

People respond quicker to warm interest and love than to criticism. When hurt and misunderstandings occur in a marital split-up, the old fears do not dissolve overnight. Indeed, they may never go away.

There are a minimum of two parties in a relationship. It takes the cooperation of both if it is to continue. If you're the willing party and the other side is not, there is little to be done to nurture such a relationship. Go on with your life.

Life isn't run by people who are experts in living. Neither are marriages. We're all beginners for the most part, doing the best we can. This means making mistakes of all kinds, of all degrees. Some can be righted by apologies or forgiveness, but many others cannot: Only time can be the healer, and not always in this lifetime.

You've got to look at yourself first, with sincerity and love. The past is past. It may not be fully in your hands to build a new future like the past. But you will be able to get a handle on your problem if you start with yourself. Be gentle and kind to yourself. We are all beginners in living.

Sex and Spirituality

What is the connection between spirituality and sex?

The deep relationship between man and woman is a sacred token of human love. The sex urge does not lift anyone into the Soul Plane, so why endorse sex as a means for spiritual unfoldment?

This relationship between a couple must be open and clean, without guilt or shame. If you cannot love your family, how will you then love God? The dirt and guilt that the orthodox religions put upon lovemaking is for control of the followers. Guilt and fear have been deeply impressed upon them for centuries.

If you cannot love your family, how will you then love God?

Lovemaking, a deep expression of love and warmth between a man and woman, is their private business. Overindulgence in anything is lust. Will we be pulled down to the common level of the animal?

The union between man and woman demands mutual responsibility. The ECK Masters advocate virginity until marriage, but I do not intrude into your private life to judge your personal relationships.

Staying a Virgin until Marriage

Why is virginity until marriage suggested by the ECK Masters?

First of all, it is a suggestion, not an order. A young person is in intensive training the first eighteen or more years of his life, learning the responsibility of self-discipline that is needed for him to be self-supporting in the world.

There is a time and a place for everything. It is natural for us to chafe against the rules that hinder our freedom. But society puts restraints on us until we learn what consequences we will shoulder for certain actions. Ignorance is no excuse under the Law of Karma.

When one is an infant, he is often a self-centered, selfish person. Because he is helpless, he is used to the world catering to his whims. All the baby has to do is cry or whine to get attention. Of course, sometime between infancy and adulthood, the individual learns that he's got the workings of the world backward: He is to serve life; life does not serve him. Until this lesson hits home, he is not understanding the purpose of Soul's reincarnation, which is to become a Co-worker with God.

Unless there is love, life can be a miserable and sad experience: an unnecessary detour on the road to God.

Virginity is suggested for the youth because without a fair grounding in life, an individual is hollow inside and mistakes sex for love. Sex takes, love gives. Unless there is love, life can be a miserable and sad experience: an unnecessary detour on the road to God.

Also, consider this: How can a child raise a child?

People of every society have rules of conduct. These rules say what is right or wrong in that society. Men, women, and children are to obey its rules for the sake of order. The ECK Masters uphold all just laws.

Let's look at a child in society. The child must first learn to care for itself. Today, that often means learning to read and write, do simple chores, make meals, and to clean up after oneself. Later, it also means finding a job.

A baby starts life with no skills at all. It begins to pick up some easy skills as a child. The harder ones come later when it is a young adult. The harder skills are learning to get along with others, even when you don't get your way.

The harder skills are learning to get along with others, even when you don't get your way.

Being born means having to learn to care for ourselves in a society. Each of us must learn how.

But could a ten-year-old girl raise a baby in most parts of the world? I think not, because the girl is herself a child. At what age would she be a good mother? And when does a boy become a man, fit for the duties of being a father? Is it ten, fifteen, or what? Each society has its own rules about that.

So your question is really about being a mature person in society.

WHEN YOUR CHILDREN ARE HURTING

My son is a very sensitive child; I guess it is difficult for him to live and function on this earth. School is very stressful for him. As a result, he is now in the hospital for treatment. How can I help him?

Your son is indeed a wise person in a little boy's body. The experience of thoughtless and cruel children at his school is not in his previous experience, nor to his liking because it is so senseless. Nevertheless, if he could be made to understand the rich opportunity he has as Soul in a human body, he might be able to face the stress. But he needs help, since he's not able to help himself in important areas.

Could the doctors recommend a different school that would have a more restful atmosphere? If your son will talk about it, ask him if he would like to go to another school. He is too sensitive for the give and take found at a regular school.

Remember that your son as Soul will and must finally decide what he wants out of this life, if anything.

Please help me understand why my children were born with so many physical problems. I love them dearly, but it saddens me and is a great strain on my marriage. Is it a strong karmic pattern we will have to live with for a long time?

The greatest thing we can possibly gain from this life is the ability to love, and to love greatly.

When we are in the lifetime where we may reach into the higher states of consciousness, past bonds of love are brought into the present so we can resolve them. The greatest thing we can possibly gain from this life is the ability to love, and to love greatly. The Holy Spirit, the ECK, brings to us whatever we need and, especially, those who need us and whom we need to fulfill our goal of reaching the richness of love.

Your children have come to you because of your great capacity to give love. And as you can give love, it increases in you. Few will understand the ECK's way of joining you with the richness of love. But in love is life.

No matter what comes, remember that the Mahanta is with you in everything. He is giving you the love so you can give it to your own.

My son is constantly in a terrible financial bind.

Things go well for him for a while, then the bottom drops out. He has a wife and three sons. I supported him for a while after his first marriage, but that didn't work out either. Maternal love is one of the biggest traps of the negative power. My nature is to leap in to help, but I am trying to see what the lesson is in all of this.

It's hard to be a parent and let our grown-up children learn the consequences of their own actions. We help as long as they learn and it helps them move forward. But there comes a time when we must look out for our own welfare. Who will look out for us when we are unable to do it ourselves?

It's time you took care of your own needs, because it's unlikely that your children will be able to help you.

We love them as much as ever. But they also must learn something: life gives us everything we need, but we must learn to accept its gifts and not turn them away.

> *Life gives us everything we need, but we must learn to accept its gifts and not turn them away.*

Your Children's Experiences

I encourage my child to share his dreams and experiences with me, if he wants to, because I want to help him understand the spiritual side of his life. However, lately I wonder if I should ask him to be silent about his experiences and establish inner discipline.

Talk with him, if he wants to talk. This sets a pattern for him to rely on the inner dreams and remember them.

When a Loved One Dies

My husband died suddenly while I was away at work. It was a great shock to me, and I feel terrible that I was not there when he went. Can you help me understand why this happened?

Your husband had finished learning what he had set out to learn in this lifetime. All the struggles within him to understand how he stood with God are resolved. It's his choice whether to serve God on the higher planes or to return to earth at a later time. For the time being he is quite satisfied on the Soul Plane, for there are many regions left to explore there.

It will be possible to meet with him via the dream state or Soul Travel if you have a strong desire to do so.

Please do not feel guilty that you were not at home during his translation from this physical life. It was the way he wanted it, to spare you from things he knew at the end, but which would not have been possible to explain to another. He is happy.

You will miss him, of course, because the absence of loved ones in the physical leaves one empty at first. But in six months you will look back at yourself and be surprised at how well you have adjusted to this very great change in your life.

My daughter was killed in a car accident. The roads were slick and she was driving fast, when her car went off a bridge. It has not been easy for me, for we were so very close.

Even though on the path of ECK we clearly know that Soul lives always, we still miss those close to us when they leave.

Even though on the path of ECK we clearly know that Soul lives always, we still miss those close to us when they leave.

Your daughter, in the Soul state, chose to end this chapter of life in order to begin one that offered her more opportunity for God Consciousness. The one trait she had that matters more than anything is love. Her love for life is so great that she needed more room to express it as a channel for God.

You also know that she continues to live and love in the other worlds. It is always possible for you to meet her when the occasion is right. The affinity between you will remain strong because your love for God is strong. Her new life will offer her opportunities that will be a joy for her to learn.

My husband whom I love dearly died yesterday. He had cancer, but I don't believe he suffered much pain at the end. I know you were there with him. He had wanted very strongly to talk with you by telephone several days ago, but when we called you were not there. I wrote you, but perhaps you didn't get the letter in time. That is my only regret, that he did not get to speak with you.

You will be able to meet each other in the dream state.

Your husband is in good hands, and you will be able to meet each other in the dream state, so you both have time to adjust to the idea of his translation from the body.

A letter from me would have made these events stretch out over several more months, giving him false hopes of recovery. He'd completed the spiritual growth he'd come to earth to do, and Soul heard the call of ECK, the Holy Spirit, and was ready for new shores.

Soul heard the call of ECK, the Holy Spirit, and was ready for new shores.

Love transcends all borders. Your love for each other will endure. The point is that you must now let yourself heal. Crying is a good physician. Please look for me on the inner planes for comfort—that is, look to the Mahanta, which is the spiritual part of myself.

The tenderness of your love for each other will

remain after the sorrow is gone. By all means, keep your love moving out to others; do not become introverted.

Why do our loved ones have to die? I feel so angry at God.

The passing of a loved one may be a time of sorrow, when we are apt to say, "Dear God, why my beloved?" We understand the order of life, which requires all people to pass to a higher place of existence. But when a loved one goes, we just don't understand.

Impatience and anger will no more bring our loved ones back to us than would patience or love, but these last two qualities can bring us healing.

The Truth about Twins

Soul cannot be split or divided. It is a complete unit of God.

I would like to know about twins. Are they two Souls or only one?

They are two Souls occupying two bodies. Soul cannot be split or divided. It is a complete unit of God.

Anger in Families

I argue all the time with myself and my family. I've tried exercises and positive thoughts, but I keep on arguing anyway. What should I do?

We get into arguments because we don't like the rules put on us. We feel that somebody has put us in a prison and there is no way out.

The ECK has you in your family because it is the best place for you to learn the customs of society. This sort of discipline gets you ready for the next level of growth and freedom. The ECK won't let us take shortcuts if it would hurt us. We get just the right experience, and not a bit more.

To get in control of your anger, try to catch yourself in the middle of an argument. Then chant HU, the holy name for God, softly to yourself. Let the argument run its natural course, just to see what it does to you. Suddenly you are surprised to find you are now in control of whether to argue or not, instead of being a helpless victim of your mind. Try this, and see how it works.

The ECK won't let us take shortcuts if it would hurt us.

HELPING OTHERS IN YOUR FAMILY

My sister is always being teased in school. Whenever she tells me and my mother about it, I get an inner nudge to say something to help her feel better. But I can never think of anything to say. Do you know of something I can say or do?

There are two reasons people tease each other: they either like someone or they don't. A boy may tease a girl because he likes her. It's a way he gets her to notice him. If this is what's happening to your sister, just say, "Aw, it's because he likes you." A girl may also cause others to tease her. What's your sister doing to get teased?

Sometimes classmates tease somebody who gets angry over nothing. They try to get an angry person mad. All you can tell her then is this, "Stop getting mad, and they won't have anything to tease you about." Sometimes a child is teased because others are jealous of him or her. This often happens to a child who is very smart or pretty. Then the best thing to do is to smile and try to make a light joke of it. But don't get angry. That just makes it worse.

Can You Love Your Family Too Much?

What is homesickness? Why do some people have it, and others not?

Homesickness hits those who love too much. It is really attachment, a too-strong bond to family and friends while separated from them. It strikes people who are overly loyal, some idealists, and homebodies. There is nothing bad about homesickness, but when a mental passion like that causes misery, the individual would be better off reconsidering his values. Human, never divine, love accounts for homesickness.

What hides behind attachment? The fear of loss. What can overcome such fear? Divine love.

What hides behind attachment? The fear of loss. What can overcome such fear? Divine love.

Questions about God

My seven-year-old son has asked me when God started. I have told him God is without beginning or end, but he wants to go to the time God started, in a time-travel machine. How do I answer his questions?

The questions from your son have been on my mind for some time. Children do want to know the ultimate mysteries of God, sometimes astounding adults who pass them off as foolish.

Tell your son that the Mahanta, the Inner Master, will have to show him why God did not start like everything else. To do this, help him draw a time machine on a piece of paper — one that satisfies him as being a worthy space vessel to undertake such a noble venture. Tell him to think of his time-travel machine at bedtime and ask the Mahanta to show him what he needs to know about

God. If this is the will of the ECK, he will find the need for that question to be fulfilled.

LIGHT BODIES

I am twelve years old. I was walking in the hallway of my house when I thought I saw a body of light in front of me. My mind said it was just because I was in a dark hallway, entering a brightly lit room. But the next time I had to go down the hallway, I got scared. Was there really a Light body in my hallway?

There are always Light bodies around us. The Astral Plane, the plane of emotions, is at a level of vibration just above the Physical Plane, but sometimes there are dips or drops in vibration. Then people catch a glimpse of the neighboring plane.

Right now, on the Astral Plane, there is a twelve-year-old girl who also thinks she saw someone in the hallway.

When you walk in your hallway, chant HU, the holy name for God. Then whisper to her, "I didn't mean to frighten you either." Don't worry, I'll be with you.

THE GOODNESS OF ECK

My two-year-old son has suddenly become afraid and distressed about singing HU. In the past he liked the HU and even sang HU to his stuffed animals. Now he asks us not to sing HU with him. I don't know what to do.

While often such a turnabout in a two-year-old can be a reaction to something on the inner planes, it may simply be linked to physical pain. For instance, a toothache. Since he can't express himself well, he rejects something he knows you regard as

The Astral Plane, the plane of emotions, is at a level of vibration just above the Physical Plane, but sometimes there are dips or drops in vibration. Then people catch a glimpse of the neighboring plane.

both good and important. Later, as the pain lessens, his reaction to HU will also reduce.

But it depends upon how the parents respond when the child rejects an important value of the family, like the teachings of ECK. He'll remember your reaction and may use it in the future as a way to control you. Children do that.

Be compassionate to his pain, but be *firm* about the goodness of ECK.

When Children See Their Past

My four-year-old daughter wakes up every night screaming and crying. It goes on for hours. She can't tell us what's wrong, and we have tried everything we can think of to help her. I am afraid. Can you help?

Sometimes a child may not be able to handle the influences of her past lives as they appear in her dreams.

Sometimes a child may not be able to handle the influences of her past lives as they appear in her dreams. In this case, I would suggest you find a counselor to help her deal with her inner problems. It's important to find a caring and sensitive person. Ask your family doctor to refer you to such a counselor, if possible.

Divine Spirit uses all kinds of doctors and healing to let us have a better life. Accept the guidance of the ECK to help you find a counselor for your daughter.

Sharing a Dream

Are the friends and family members I meet in my dreams actually sharing the experience? Is it as real for them as it is for me (though they may not remember)? Or are they only present as mock-ups in my mind?

You may all have the same dream experience. Yet there are times when your mind will create a fantasy world, like a dramatist who moves characters around in a play. How do you tell the difference? What is illusion, what is truth?

The key is the Spiritual Exercises of ECK. They help you sort out the real experiences from the false ones.

Some people tell other people about their dreams in order to control others. For example, a man tells a woman about his dream where she agreed to marry him. It's a choke hold. His intentions should stand on their own merits. That means he should simply say he loves her. Then it's up to her to decide whether the relationship holds anything for her without the pressure of trying to live up to his dream.

As I've said before—the inner life is for the inner, the outer life is for the outer.

It's unfair to others to say they've agreed to something that happened in your dreams. You may have been under a spell of illusion.

Each person has many dream experiences every night, and no one can remember them all later. So just as others don't remember their place in your dreams, you are likely to draw a blank on your role in theirs.

Each recalls the events that strike his or her imagination.

The key is the Spiritual Exercises of ECK. They help you sort out the real experiences from the false ones.

LEARNING ABOUT LIFE

Who do you listen to if your inner guidance tells you that something is all right for you to do, but your parent or someone else deserving of respect tells you that you may not?

That depends upon what our so-called inner guidance tells us to do. The guidance may be from the negative force, instead of from the Mahanta. The whole purpose of the teachings of ECK is to teach us the difference.

Growing up, spiritually and physically, means that more and more people are affected by what we do. When a four-year-old boy hits his younger brother on the head with his hand, his parents see no great harm is done, because the child has so little strength. Therefore, the child gets a mild rebuke.

But let's say the child grows up. Now he's fifteen. He strikes a classmate in a fit of anger and hurts him. Will his punishment be as light as when he was a child? Again, it depends upon what provoked his anger—belligerence or self-defense.

Most people make impulsive decisions while under the control of the passions of the mind. This has nothing to do with the inner guidance of the Mahanta. They are selfish human beings who think only of their own gratification. In this case, they must suffer the consequences of their runaway emotions.

There's a hard way and an easy way to learn about life.

There's a hard way and an easy way to learn about life. If you've ever tried a new game in the video arcade, you can lose a handful of quarters in no time while trying to learn the game by yourself. A better way is to watch someone who has played the game before and imitate him.

Parents and teachers are role models for us. They do not have all the answers, but they are responsible for their children's entry into society as mature individuals. If they cannot do the job, then the negative force sees to it that the courts limit the destructive behavior of their children.

The older you become, the more you find there

is no right or wrong in an absolute sense. The guiding rule that will stand you well throughout life is this ECK saying: Is it true, is it necessary, is it kind? Unless the answer is yes for all three, then you would do well to reconsider your intended action.

That saying will resolve many of the problems that are facing you now in trying to understand the conflict you feel between your inner guidance and the guidance of your parents and others.

AGE OF SENSITIVITY

I have a lot of trouble in my room. I am fourteen years old and still have nightmares or see things, such as a ghost. I do a visualization technique in which I put ECK Masters around the windows and doors, but it doesn't always work. I still get afraid. What can I do?

You're at an age of high sensitivity. It can take the form of nightmares or seeing ghosts, a problem that my sister and I also ran into from about the age of twelve to fifteen.

A small night-light or two for your bedroom is a way to keep the powers of night at bay. Another is to have a pet in your room overnight. And keep up the spiritual exercises. Don't watch horror shows on TV at all, but try to watch upbeat programs of comedy, nature, or sports. Many soft drinks are high in caffeine, which makes for tense nerves—so replace harmful soft drinks with teas or fruit drinks. Take multivitamins and multiminerals. Be sure to get enough rest and exercise.

The above suggestions can bring you more calm. Put extra attention on peace and quiet for another year or two, after which your sensitivity will balance out.

The guiding rule that will stand you well throughout life is this ECK saying: Is it true, is it necessary, is it kind?

FAMILY HARMONY

*I would like to become a member of Eckankar,
but my parents don't want me to. I am in high school
now. What can I do?*

For the present time it is better to study and read
the books of Eckankar rather than considering membership. I like to keep families together. It's best for
a person to reach legal age before considering membership unless the rest of the family are already
members.

If you find a spiritual exercise in one of the ECK
books that you would like to do on your own, until you
are earning your own way, you are certainly welcome
to do so. If you want to practice the Easy Way technique
or another exercise in the Eckankar book called *The
Spiritual Exercises of ECK,* you will find the love and
protection of the Mahanta are always with you.

I can understand your hunger for truth. But remember that the ECK actually keeps families together and does not separate them. As long as you
are in your parents' home, it is more honest to respect
their wishes that you not join the outer membership
of Eckankar.

I do not want to see a family quarrel about ECK.
We try to live as quietly, discreetly, and harmoni-
ously with our kin as possible. There is no advantage
in making our beliefs the center of controversy at
home. Parents have a duty to society to raise their
children in the way that's right for them, and I
cannot interfere.

*If you want
to practice
the Easy Way
technique or
another
exercise in
the Eckankar
book called
The Spiritual
Exercises of
ECK, you
will find the
love and
protection of
the Mahanta
are always
with you.*

RESPONSIBILITY

*Like other youth, decisions await me about how
to handle responsibilities—either in career, in college,*

or in personal relationships. I see responsibility as another face of love. But is there a way to tell if I'm using responsibility as an excuse to avoid experiences?

Responsibility is a big word, and it can frighten us. It tries to take a snapshot of us running through life and put a caption to this single picture, which is so small compared to all life that it's nearly invisible.

But what does a word like that tagged on to what we do after it's done mean? As you say, responsibility is another face of love. Every time a decision faces you, the question is: "Will you be responsible or not?" But responsible to whom?

The usual definition of responsibility is what society expects of you, but that may not always be the right thing to do. At the crossroads of decision, ask the Inner Master what to do. He will tell you by intuition, by knowing, or by direct speech what decision is spiritually correct.

At the crossroads of decision, ask the Inner Master what to do.

For now, get experiences in work, in education, in your spiritual exercises, and in your personal relationships. When you turn decisions over to the Mahanta, this expression of the Spirit of God that is always with you, you will do the responsible thing. The point is to live life with a loving, grateful heart.

HAVING PERSONAL FREEDOMS

I'm having trouble with my life. I am tired of everything I'm doing. It always feels like I am following someone else's rules rather than a natural extension of my own spiritual nature. Where is the freedom I want from life?

I can appreciate your frustration. You have so

much energy but haven't found a place to put it to use or how.

Something that bothered me in college was the fact of having to tell somebody so early what classes I wanted to take that would fit my career plans. I had no plans. There was so much freedom and so much energy, but I didn't know what to do with my life.

Then the U.S. got into Vietnam. The draft board helped me make a decision: better to join the Air Force than be drafted into the Army and land in Vietnam. I lost some freedom in service, but the Air Force taught me skills and gave me direction in life.

You have youth, health, and energy. If you can marshal your self-discipline, the world is at your feet. You have many things to be grateful for, despite all the uncertainty.

You have many things to be grateful for, despite all the uncertainty.

DRUGS—A SPIRITUAL DEAD END

As a teen, I wonder, Where is one when one is on drugs?

Drugs are a rose-lined lane to misery and unhappiness. I can't say this strongly enough.

Few who dabble in drugs want to admit that there is any danger in using them. They use them to escape boredom, and boredom itself is a crime against the creative power of Soul.

Every act has a consequence, so are we ready to pay the piper?

Drugs bring unreal experiences in the elementary Astral world—some good, some bad, but all petty. What good ever comes from putting our sanity on the line for little pills and powders?

How do you say no to "friends" who push drugs at you? That happened to me in a house where I once lived with thirteen other people. I just said no. God Consciousness was my goal, and I did not want to turn into a druggie like them.

Have you ever noticed the cute names the negative force has put on drugs? You know most of them—angel dust, coke, buttons, smack or horse, orange sunshine, and the like. The cute labels are to hide the horror that catches Soul once It falls for them. Drugs are a shortcut to more unbearable incarnations, and they hardly bring more than simple light and color, at best.

Chant HU if you want to see the negative force's face behind the face of a "friend" who pushes drugs at you. Soul Travel is better—it puts you in control of your life and is completely safe. Soul Travel is the natural way for expansion of consciousness and travel into the spiritual worlds of God.

Soul Travel is the natural way for expansion of consciousness and travel into the spiritual worlds of God.

CLEANING UP YOUR ACT

What happens to those who use foul language? I hear it all the time at school, and I want to understand the consequences of it.

Foul language, no matter how you spell it, is for the barnyard. The simple ECK principle is this: where your attention is, so are you. What you hold in your thoughts is what you become.

Since you're an expression of the Sound and Light of God, do you want to bring beauty, joy, love, and harmony to the world? Then choose words that do that. The words you speak are an expression of what you are and what you'd like to be.

What you hold in your thoughts is what you become.

Almost every day people come up to me and speak negatively of someone, or I hear people around me gossiping. I have noticed that even when I do not support what they are saying, they lower my opinion about that individual.

What can I do to avoid getting involved in this gossip?

Once when I was a freshman in high school, four of my roommates were gossiping about our other roommate. Their comments were sharp, biting, and largely untrue.

I was only half listening to them but noticed, as you have, that their opinions were having a bad effect on me. Suddenly, these words dropped from my lips: "Won't anybody here speak up for Bill?"

All four turned to glare at me. It was very uncomfortable, because I had not meant to embarrass anyone, especially since two of them were sophomores. But my question broke up the group. After that, they chose their words more carefully around me.

Was it courage that had made me speak up for Bill? In a way, yes. The Mahanta had given me the words to speak, but I had to speak them. The Mahanta was already guiding me then, years before I had first heard of Eckankar.

This may not work in your case. But listen to the Inner Master the next time such an occasion arises, and you will know what to do or say.

The Mahanta was already guiding me then, years before I had first heard of Eckankar.

Discrimination and Inner Guidance

How can someone tell whether he is being guided by the ECK or by the mind?

You can't ever be sure.

Why?

The mind has a power to make you believe you

are always right. That's why a headstrong person acts so smart. He thinks he's always right, though he's often wrong.

So, then, what is the good of ECK?

If guided by the ECK, the Holy Spirit, we are more likely to change our minds when new information comes along. We're quicker to admit that an earlier decision based on sketchy information needs to change. Those under the guidance of the ECK are always alert. The purpose of the ECK is to have each individual at the peak of awareness.

MISTAKES OF THE PAST

When I was a child of eight, I stole food from my father. This was during the war when food was as precious as life. Now I am an adult and have great fear of being called a thief. How can I reconcile these mistakes of my youth and free myself of this shame? I am now twenty-nine and working as a lawyer in our small town.

Let the mistakes of your youth remain in the past. Everyone has things in the past he would like to forget. What is important, however, is that you've done something to improve yourself. Through the practice of law and your experiences as a youth, you can be a better and more useful Co-worker with the Mahanta.

Be fair in your dealings with people, and you can do much good.

ANGER

I'm a thirteen-year-old boy. How can I learn to control my temper and stop fighting with my brother?

Those under the guidance of the ECK are always alert. The purpose of the ECK is to have each individual at the peak of awareness.

A big reason for anger at your age is that you want to have more freedom in every way, to get more independence to do what you want and not what others tell you to do.

The anger comes because we think we know more than we do. But important lessons that lie ahead during the next few years include: What knowledge do you need to prepare you to leave home after high school? How much do you have to meet halfway the opinions of coworkers in order to have a life filled with rich spiritual adventures and growth?

The parents' duty is to give their children a firm foundation in the spiritual principles, so we can learn ways to live in harmony with people around us, including brothers. Get into some sport you like a lot to work off some energy, and go into contemplation for the rest of the answer to your question.

TELLING RIGHT FROM WRONG

Any act that holds someone else or yourself back is wrong, whether you say you are doing it in the name of God or not.

If you do something wrong, but do it in the name of God, is it still wrong? Like if you're with friends and doing drugs, but doing it in the name of God?

Drugs, in any case, don't help you out. They are stopping you on the most direct way to God.

Any act that holds someone else or yourself back is wrong, whether you say you are doing it in the name of God or not. The words don't make it right.

COMPETITION

Is it unspiritual to like games such as chess, since the very nature of such games is based on war, power, and egotistical competition?

Not in my opinion. This is a warring universe.

To survive here, one must know its ways.

Chess is simply another way an individual can test his survival instinct. Competition is not necessarily a bad activity. It forms the very basis of many societies today. Their members must know how to move in such an environment and how to provide a protective shield (a home, for example) for themselves and their families.

Competition is all right as long as a person develops and follows a code of fair play.

GETTING GUIDANCE

Have you ever listened to the guidance of Divine Spirit, followed it, then watched everything go wrong afterward? I wonder if sometimes I misunderstood what I got.

Divine Spirit wants you to learn and have experiences. The result may not be what you want but it's helping you learn and grow.

It's not what happens to you but your attitude about what happens that's really important. When something happens to you, ask, Since this is what Spirit got for me, what does it mean? How is it helping me grow?

When something happens to you, ask, Since this is what Spirit got for me, what does it mean? How is it helping me grow?

GIVING OTHERS FREEDOM

Can I use spiritual methods to get someone to be my friend?

You mean if you wanted someone to be your friend, could you make that happen?

A better way is to let the person have complete freedom to make up his or her mind. You don't really want a friend who doesn't want you. It never works. But you can be a good friend by allowing others space.

Anyone who is worth his weight likes freedom, and as soon as we take away the freedom the person doesn't like us anymore. It causes a lot of heartache for us. Friendship has to be two-way.

Soul Just Is

Did God create all Souls at the same time? If yes, why? And if not, why not?

In our world, we must think about time. Even your question says "at the same time." But God, also known as Sugmad in the ancient teachings, created Souls before time began, so it is not a question of Souls made sooner or later. As humans, we find this hard to understand.

Yet even when studying the origin of this universe, scientists run into a problem of how to determine the age of the "big bang." It's a theory about the moment of creation. But creation happened before there was time. So scientists work from there and accept the fact of creation, because the evidence is all around. However, they cannot fix a date to the beginning of time. It's simply not possible.

Sugmad created all Souls before time began, so there is no answer to your question of when. If God creates more Souls, that also happens beyond the laws of time and space.

Soul just is.

We know that Soul exists by the evidence of life around us. When Soul inhabits a body, that body lives, moves, and has being. When Soul leaves, the body no longer lives, moves, or has being. What has

When Soul inhabits a body, that body lives, moves, and has being. When Soul leaves, the body no longer lives, moves, or has being.

left? By direct and indirect evidence, we know that some unseen force gives life to a physical body.

What is that something? Soul, of course.

There is no simple reply to your question. But spiritually, there is an answer. In contemplation, ask the Mahanta to let you see and know about the creation and nature of Soul. If you are sincere, he will show you.

The most important point of all is that you are Soul. Know that you are a spark of God and can exist fully only within the realization of that profound truth. As such, you are a light and inspiration to others.

Know that you are a spark of God and can exist fully only within the realization of that profound truth.

The teachings of ECK are to give us ideas: how we can approach our problems in ways that bring a degree of peace and contentment.

7

CREATIVITY AND SELF-DISCIPLINE

I still cannot manifest things in my life that I desire. I have guilt feelings because I don't have any self-discipline. Before, I didn't depend on anyone but myself, but along the way, I lost this mastery of self. Please show me how to break this stalemate.

It was good to hear from you even though life has got you down. As you said, it is hard to overcome the inertia that prevents self-discipline. The teachings of ECK are to give us ideas: how we can approach our problems in ways that bring a degree of peace and contentment.

Most important in the spiritual works of ECK is the knowledge that a solution to every problem is within us.

The human consciousness can act like a pit of quicksand, always pulling us down relentlessly. The spiritual exercises are the linkup to Divine Spirit. They are a rope we can use to pull ourselves free from this sort of despondency.

What is our goal? Manifesting material things is not the goal of saints, although most start out trying

The spiritual exercises are the linkup to Divine Spirit.

to accomplish this as a first step. The biblical saying is true in that we seek first the Kingdom of God and all things shall be added to us.

The cycle of creative action begins with the concept we carry in our minds of what we wish to do. The next step is to outline on paper some plan of how to accomplish this. The final step is action in carrying out the plan.

This is the mysterious Rule of Threes that lies behind every successful creative venture. Another way of saying this is that a project must be seen in the light of three essential elements: the positive, the negative, and the unseen but essential neutralizing element still undiscovered by science as the catalyst.

Set your plans up in some structure of threes because that is the formula that embodies the creative principle.

Set your plans up in some structure of threes because that is the formula that embodies the creative principle.

SPIRITUAL SELF-DISCIPLINE

I often hear those on the path of ECK describe very personal experiences. This makes me wonder, What constitutes the Law of Silence?

The Law of Silence is a spiritual principle that draws a very fine line. If you have an experience that may help another person understand his own, then tell it in a fitting way.

Also be sure that telling your experience will really help that person. Sometimes we like to brag about our imagined superior spiritual development.

You can tell when you've said too much: Your stomach will knot up; you'll feel uncomfortable. It takes some people a long time to learn to watch their own bodies as a sensitivity meter about how their words affect others. But you can learn to do it.

The Law of Silence is easier to learn if you're more willing to just listen to others instead of having to pummel them with your great wisdom.

Someone once said, "Life's too short to make all the mistakes yourself. So learn from those of others."

How can I be sure which spiritual experiences should not be discussed?

The way of ECK is one of experience. Use the trial-and-error method to see which inner experiences are too sacred for public discussion.

Keep track of your inner experiences for a given period of time and talk of them to your usual confidants. What happens is that the Mahanta begins to shut down the individual's memory of the sacred teachings that are given to him. Within a month or two, you will become aware that the golden hand of the Mahanta's love and protection has been withdrawn. You will feel empty and alone.

When you are convinced of the emptiness that comes of giving the secret teachings of the Mahanta to those who have no right to them, then make it a practice to keep all the inner happenings to yourself. It will take one to two months before the channel to the ECK will open you to the secret teachings again.

This experiment can be done as often as needed. Finally, your self-discipline and spiritual discrimination becomes such that you know which inner experiences can be shared to help others and which are for you alone.

Use the trial-and-error method to see which inner experiences are too sacred for public discussion.

RESISTING DOWNWARD PULLS

I have a craving for narcotics, which are at my disposal as a nurse. I'm feeling very angry at myself and guilty. Help!

The pull of drugs and alcohol is almost more than one can shake off by himself. Consider exploring a drug-abuse program that will not jeopardize your nursing career. Divine Spirit helps us when we take the first step ourselves.

The ECK Masters have had to face every test in their struggle for the God Consciousness. The divine promise of Soul is that every problem contains a solution. The key is self-discipline and surrender of the mental habits to the ECK.

What can help me break the hold of depression? I find myself very dispirited about my marriage and life in general.

Lift yourself above negativity through the Easy Way technique.

There are several ways to break the negative hold that you have upon you. One is to lift yourself above this negativity through a spiritual exercise. For this I recommend the Easy Way technique.

Just before going to bed at night place your attention on the Spiritual Eye, that place between the eyebrows. Chant HU or God inwardly and silently.

Hold your attention on a blank screen in the inner vision, and keep it free of any pictures if at all possible. If you need a substitute for mental pictures flashing up unwantedly, put the image of the Living ECK Master in place of them.

Do this spiritual exercise for fifteen or twenty minutes a day. It generally won't happen overnight, but when the time is right, you will begin to see lights, usually blue or white. You will then be led to the next step within your own worlds.

When you are ready, you will find the peace, comfort, and joy that come from the illumination of God.

The second part is to get counseling. Try the Family Service Association that is listed in the phone book. This is a positive step because the people there are willing to help you find the next step in your life.

The whole point about Soul incarnating in the world is so that It can master every situation that develops in Its life. This is self-mastery. We arrange our lives so that we come into harmony with the laws of Divine Spirit. Whatever decision we make, it is done in the name of the ECK. It results in good for everyone concerned.

There is no way to bow out of life and think we've cheated our due lessons. It may sound harsh, but the troubles we have are of our own making. Furthermore, the solution to all trouble also lies within the abilities of Soul to rise above and work from the whole viewpoint. This comes through the expansion of consciousness that is attained through faithful practice of the Spiritual Exercises of ECK.

Divine Spirit often begins working for our welfare after we have made some small effort first. The love and protection of Spirit surround you at all times but must be accepted with a loving heart.

The whole point about Soul incarnating in the world is so that It can master every situation that develops in Its life.

I've been unable to discipline myself in the area of drugs. I feel I am trying to pursue two paths at once, the path of ECK and the path of the negative force.

You're being honest with yourself. I respect that. A spiritual path that's suitable for you will build upon your abilities and interests and lead you to God-Realization. Only you can, and should, decide what is truth for you.

A person trying to mix ECK and recreational drugs does untold damage to his own spiritual unfoldment as well as that of others. It becomes a grave spiritual violation when someone introduces another person to drugs. The Lords of Karma take that case.

DOES SMOKING AFFECT
YOUR SPIRITUAL GROWTH?

I am a truck driver and on the road most of the time. I have tried to quit smoking for many years. For a long time I have felt spiritually dead. It seems I have been rewarded materially instead of spiritually. I want so much to be a knowing spiritual being, but I feel that my smoking habit is keeping me from that. Please help.

Thanks for your letter about smoking and what seems to be a lack of spiritual progress. Someone on the path of ECK who smokes is demonstrating that his habit is more important to him than the things of Divine Spirit. Until he gives it up, the Mahanta has little to offer him in the way of spiritual gifts. Some habits, however, are deeply ingrained. No one expects them to go away immediately. What seems to be a long time to us—ten to twenty years—is only the blink of an eye for Soul.

Awareness of the moment and a joy for living can also be an indication of where you are spiritually.

You cannot measure spirituality by the number of bad habits you have or not. Nor by a certain number of experiences. Awareness of the moment and a joy for living can also be an indication of where you are spiritually.

Some, like you, are given spiritual gifts through an abundance of material goods. Appreciate those things, because they too are gifts of the ECK.

FASTING FROM BAD HABITS

What is a mental fast? How would you describe it?

A mental fast is simply putting one's attention on God for a twenty-four-hour period. Another way is to take every negative thought that comes to mind and throw it into a wastebasket.

The mental fast is important. It is done on Friday, and on that day a person thinks and acts in a refined way around others. The fast is a discipline to put one's attention upon the Inner Master. The individual who puts it there is acting in the name of the ECK. This cuts down the daily karma between himself and others.

A mental fast is simply putting one's attention on God for a twenty-four-hour period.

Spiritual students are held to account for daily karma. If a driver speeds seventy-five miles per hour in a fifty-five-mile-per-hour zone and gets caught, there is a fine to pay. No matter how one tries to fool himself that he is above the Law of Karma, the fine must be paid.

The mental fast uplifts the individual's state of consciousness by changing old mental structures and ideas. Thus he treats life with more reverence and looks at it with new eyes.

When to Take Action, When Not

I've been trying to work with another person on a team I am responsible for. But we have a hard time getting along. I have tried to surrender this to Divine Spirit, but I don't know if I am avoiding doing something I should do.

You know how to surrender to the ECK to handle your life. A person is obligated to do all he can for himself, but when his best efforts fail, then he turns the whole bundle over to Divine Spirit to see how it can be done the right way.

It is especially trying to run into somebody who tells you to your face that your way of doing things is wrong and that he will not abide by your wishes, when you are the party responsible for the handling of it.

That is a good time to step back and say, "If that's what you think is right, OK, we'll try it your way." That is, of course, provided his way is not totally off the wall.

What do I do when I hear something really awful—perhaps illegal—about someone I respect?

If someone comes to me and says, "So and so caused me injury," I tell them to gather the facts in the case and present them to the civil and criminal authorities. Let the law decide the case; the court system is the proper place for the airing of criminal and civil grievances. We support the process of due justice.

We support the process of due justice.

To act and speak about alleged misdeeds without proof or without being a principal in the case makes one subject to charges of slander or libel.

We must be careful not to let ourselves be victims of hearsay, but always encourage the *principals* to go to the civil authorities for the due process of law. Otherwise, we may ourselves be the perpetrators of a great wrong upon the innocent.

ANSWERING SPIRITUAL QUESTIONS

What's the best way to work on the inner to get answers to spiritual questions?

The Easy Way technique is given earlier in this chapter on page 150. This spiritual exercise is an opportunity in learning to rely on the Inner Master. Mentally ask your question while you're doing the

Easy Way technique and again ask it before dropping off to sleep at night. The answer will come, sometimes in an obvious manner. Other times it comes subtly—through the advice of a friend, a humorous anecdote, or as a symbolic dream that you develop the knack of interpreting for yourself.

List all your questions on a sheet of paper. A month later, review them to see if any have resolved themselves. Do this with all your questions every month and send me a report, if you like, regarding the results.

ACTION AS SELF-DISCIPLINE

What kind of self-discipline is needed to get through a particularly difficult time—such as the death of someone close?

Although one's mind pretends to understand the parting at the translation of a loved one from earth, the heart does not. Keep yourself active in the weeks ahead, for that will dim the loneliness.

PRIVILEGE OF LIFE

My husband killed himself. I feel great pain and loneliness, and so do my children. Can you help me understand why my husband did this and what I can do to heal? Why do people commit suicide?

Life simply becomes too much of a burden for some because they look for spiritual love but can't find it. They feel they have no choice but to end the impasse by taking their own life.

Your husband is in a class now so he can get a fuller understanding of the privilege of coming into a physical body for spiritual maturity. He did not

Keep yourself active in the weeks ahead, for that will dim the loneliness.

understand this. This does not mean he's put in some kind of hell for a certain time, because the spiritual structure is designed to educate, rather than punish, those people who harm themselves by suicide.

The greatest misunderstanding is thinking that a spiritual giant has to withdraw from life in order to be successful with the God Consciousness. Nothing could be further from the truth.

One can always take his life, of course. This does not lead to God, but it leads back to a baby body almost immediately. Then all the tests and trials start over again until Soul comes to know what it means to become a Co-worker with God. When people write me about this, I usually tell them to seek a trained, licensed counselor who can help them understand some of the responsibilities that go along with living.

All too often a person has damaged himself emotionally and mentally through austerities before he found the path of Eckankar, the spiritual way that teaches balance and moderation in all departments of living. By then, their only real aid must come through licensed medical and counseling practitioners.

Self-destruction is not the way. How can one leave the worlds of God?

> *The greatest misunderstanding is thinking that a spiritual giant has to withdraw from life in order to be successful with the God Consciousness.*

THE PURPOSE OF MUSIC

Do certain types of music affect people negatively? If so, how?

Let's say this: The music you like tells a lot about you. Some music is uplifting, while other music is not. Certain music is harsh, yet that does not mean it is not music. Take, for example, the music of the

Chinese, Japanese, and Indian people. It may hurt the ears of many people in the West, as does bagpipe music. Yet it is the choice of millions. So what is negative music?

Usually, it is music not to our liking.

Music can break up thought forms in a society. For example, look at the music of Elvis Presley and the Beatles. At first, the media made fun of it. That soon changed.

Music can break up thought forms in a society.

Teens' music is sure to offend parents, and vice versa. Music, like anything else, becomes very negative when we try to push our tastes off on others— like blaring our music in public. Those on the path of ECK have a high regard for the rights of others.

And yes, many people do serious harm to their ears by playing music too loudly through headsets. That is a very negative side of music—though of volume and not of kind.

WRITE DOWN YOUR EXPERIENCES

What is the purpose of writing down spiritual experiences?

You may miss the connection at first between the mission of the Living ECK Master and the life of Portugal's Henry the Navigator, of the early fifteenth century. Henry actually set up the conditions that enabled Columbus to discover America.

Until Henry's day, sea charts were closely guarded secrets. Many of them reflected errors of the clergy, whose maps tried to rest upon their understanding of the Bible. Henry changed all that.

Portugal became a country committed to exploration. Henry required the sailors to debrief after each voyage. Every bit of new travel information was incorporated into maps that marked latitude and longitude. Slowly, Portuguese sailors pushed back the walls of ignorance that enclosed the world then.

That's what the Living ECK Master is doing today: The sailors of the Cosmic Sea are recording their journeys into the unknown world beyond the physical plane.

The sailors of the Cosmic Sea are recording their journeys into the unknown world beyond the physical plane.

This is the purpose of their spiritual journals, their initiate reports, and the books and articles they write. We must compile this information in the interest of spiritual survival. Many hands will contribute to this mission as best they can.

Do you see the point?

Writing has opened up a whole new world for me. Is it possible to heal the past through what we write?

A writer's work can be a revelation to the writer. As you transcend the daily reality, it's found to be a mask that covers old feelings, old fears.

The process of writing uncovers our own deepest thoughts and emotions, then transforms them into a medium of teaching for others. We can change the future through an understanding and reconciliation of the past.

CREATIVE SUCCESS

What does it take to become really successful at a creative pursuit like writing, music, or art?

It really makes very little difference what we choose to do with our talents and interests. Life in ECK just means that we live life to the hilt.

Writing is a very difficult undertaking. If your

interest is in writing, you must immerse yourself in it. That means writing and reading a lot. Read to learn, and write to give.

Study your audience. For whom are you writing? Let's say you did a humor piece for *Reader's Digest*. What are their needs? Once you understand their needs, you can either meet them or look for another outlet that fits your style. You may have the greatest article in the world, but it's got to get past the editor before anyone in the world will read it. So, please the editor. Learn about his needs in *Writer's Market* and *Writer's Digest*.

Whatever you plan to do, find something you really want to do—and are willing to sweat and labor for without recognition. The Mahanta sometimes teaches surrender to Divine Spirit in the most down-to-earth ways.

CREATIVE CHANNELS

What roles do discipline and imagination play in being a creative vehicle for God? I would like to be a writer someday.

The classic children's book *Harold and the Purple Crayon* illustrates the creative principle of the imagination.

All success begins with the imagination that pulls together the ethereal substance. Then discipline takes the next step and plans how to bring the concept or invention down into the physical reality. This little book is a wonderful example of Soul working through Its imagination.

For those of us who labor over a typewriter or computer, this form of creative expression ranges from agony to ecstasy. When the ethereal idea reaches

The Mahanta sometimes teaches surrender to Divine Spirit in the most down-to-earth ways.

the paper in a clean, easy-to-understand way, then there is the satisfaction of having successfully made a bridge between heaven and earth.

Remember how the grade-school teacher used to make you diagram English sentences? It is a surprise to see what turns up when the same technique is used on published writers in a successful magazine. Does the writer begin with several short, catchy examples that illustrate the principle that he is about to present to you, the reader? Is the whole thing done through the story form? How is a problem given, and in what manner does the writer draw a solution?

My observation has shown that if I want to learn to do a thing well, the idea is to find somebody who is an expert in the field of my interest. This applies especially to writing.

Universities offer writing classes. This is a good way to get the discipline to start putting words on paper. It is nothing more, after all, than learning how to sit down and arrange thoughts into a step-by-step pattern that is familiar and enjoyable to the reader.

The best rule of thumb to finding a writer to use as an ideal is first of all: Does he sell? Secondly, ask yourself, Do I like his stories?

The writing style must, above all, be a simple one. Simple and alive! Let your writing have time to "cure" between rewrites. Good writing is done through rewriting.

If I want to learn to do a thing well, the idea is to find somebody who is an expert in the field of my interest.

I am a musician and would like to know the best kind of music to compose to spread Divine Spirit's message. What spiritual purpose does music have?

ECK music opens the heart of Soul.

As to what kind of music to compose: Simply,

people have to like it. A song touches many because of the beautiful melody. The dictionary says a melody is "a sweet or agreeable succession or arrangement of sounds." Depending upon the skill of the composer, that touches people.

Music has to break loose and soar somewhere in its presentation, with melody.

Listen to the ECK, the Music of God, and write what you will.

In writing, Shakespeare's works are for the highbrow today. But when he wrote them, they were popular works for the masses (like Steven Spielberg and his movies). The hot blood of life once coursed through Shakespearean plays, but the language is outmoded now. Few can understand it.

Music must be alive today if it expects to be a classic years from now. As a composer, you probably have several ideas of how to approach this challenge.

So few know what a love for living means. They've put a web around themselves and called it the Holy Spirit. Life is a celebration. Some will read that as wanton living, but true celebration is loving God and Its own.

You hear the Music. Follow It; don't lose It. Listen to the ECK, the Music of God, and write what you will.

When one gives up and lets go of his opinions about a
situation, then Divine Spirit, the ECK, will open the door
to a new spiritual vista.

8

CHANGE AND GROWTH

It is my nature to wish to know the next step before the present one is taken. Lately, I am not being given that luxury. The wind of change screams in my being, "This time you must take your ship out of sight of shore." Do you have any tips to help me know if I'm on the right track spiritually during this time of change?

Life does throw us into circumstances that are always a bit of a challenge. And nothing is so dark as when the Holy Spirit, the ECK, urges us to step into the great unknown.

From experience, I find that I'm always on the frontier of my own abilities. This proves that there is always an avenue we haven't trod: one more step to the heavenly kingdom that is in us.

Follow the ECK; see where It leads you. It is the essence of God that binds all life together. There is never any separation from It except in consciousness, so the worlds are at your feet. All that counts is what you do in them.

The worlds are at your feet. All that counts is what you do in them.

SURRENDER

What's the easiest way to bring about changes in one's life? I have been struggling for some time to improve my outer life but can't seem to figure out how to do it.

When one gives up and lets go of his opinions about a situation, then Divine Spirit, the ECK, will open the door to a new spiritual vista. You will find that when you allow changes to occur on the inner planes, there are also changes in the outer life.

Each step in the higher worlds must be earned in some manner. Ultimately, however, it is simply a matter of surrender to the Inner Master, which is the ECK.

You will find that when you allow changes to occur on the inner planes, there are also changes in the outer life.

Doubt's Role

What is the role of doubt?

Doubt provides a stabilizing factor that prevents one from going too fast in the spiritual works and losing control. The Mahanta pulls the curtain on the memory, oftentimes, of experiences in the Light and Sound of God. The shock would be too great and throw us into emotional disorders, as happened to certain saints who briefly tasted the love of God.

If a hockey player or baseball team didn't practice their sport, they could not compete in the league. They must play or practice their sport daily during the season in order to meet the competition and be successful. The same with the Spiritual Exercises of ECK. You build spiritual stamina by practicing them daily for twenty to thirty minutes. And in doing so, you find doubts resolve themselves very naturally in a way that is best for you.

Fear of Change

Although I have a great love for the ECK, there have always been times of uncertainty and fear of change. Sometimes I fear that, even with all my hope, love, and dedication, I might fall. I do not want to fail myself or God. Where is the assurance that we can be guided back if we go astray?

Your concerns about failing to reach God-Realization are well taken. Life is uncertain, especially when we use outer signs to judge our inner state of consciousness.

There never can be failure in our quest for the Divine Awareness if we absolutely fix our complete attention upon the Sound and Light of God. The trouble comes when we slip off our spiritual center and become concerned with outer relationships— and then let this concern reflect back into our inner worlds and distort our spiritual reality.

No matter what outer events arise to throw us off our spiritual center, we must return to the Sound and Light. We must lock on to them as the only things certain of our trust.

Life is acknowledged to be a stormy sea. Yet so often when the boat rocks, we fly into a panic, as if a boat shouldn't rock in a storm.

The storms of life separate the cosmic sailors from the meek landlubbers. Look always to the Light and Sound of God within you, and you will always sail the cosmic sea.

Cycles of Change

I feel a sort of sadness when one cycle ends in my life and another begins. Can you explain this?

Life teaches that all living beings go through cycles of change. This does not mark the end of your spiritual opportunities but another beginning.

Soul operates in cycles of activity and rest. The

The storms of life separate the cosmic sailors from the meek landlubbers.

ECK sees, and indeed sets, the grand design of our lives and gives us choices that we accept and grow from.

A good thought might be, Hold fast to the ECK, but let go of those things that pass. In that light, you will never stand in your own way.

Living can be a joy. It should give us a sense of wonder and love.

Living can be a joy. It should give us a sense of wonder and love.

WHAT MISTAKES MEAN

I have always been afraid of making mistakes. I can't seem to let go of this attitude. Can you help?

Learning means making errors. Those who are learning spiritually make errors just the way anyone does when he is growing.

I don't mind an error as long as the individual benefits from it, picks up the pieces, and goes on— a wiser individual.

FEAR OF DEATH

I am eighty-seven years old and not a member of Eckankar. I am asking if you could help break the terrible fear of death I have carried with me since childhood. I want to have this burden gone forever and the assurance that someone will meet me when my time comes. I want it to be the beautiful experience it was meant to be.

Please be assured that your loved ones will meet you on the other side, so there's no reason to hold on to your fear.

If you'll keep in mind that love and love alone is the reason for living, it will calm your heart and free you from your worries. And, of course, I am always with you in my spiritual self.

Surviving a Great Loss

Our five-year-old daughter passed on unexpect-edly. She lit up my life to a degree I cannot describe. My son says she came to teach us about love. I would like to believe that my love for her is the love of God. Please help us during these difficult times.

The hand of sorrow has touched your family deeply. The wisdom of your son is right: Your daughter came to teach you all to love each other more.

We understand that life is a series of comings and goings, but somehow the passing of a child is harder to accept than is the passing of one well along in years. It is hard to see now, but life will replace the joy you have lost with even greater joy. But first you must heal your sorrow, and that will take time.

Your daughter came to teach you all to love each other more.

Any words I write to you about the loss of your daughter cannot heal the ache of your heart. I would suggest that in contemplation you ask to meet the Mahanta as a family, including your daughter, of course. You will receive the understanding you need about human love being the link to love for God and the Mahanta.

I am with you in your days of sorrow, and I will remain with you in the happier days to come. This I promise you. Look for the Light, listen for the Sound—in your heart.

Helping Others with Grief

How can I help a Christian friend whose child recently died?

It would help first to understand the consciousness of people in this Christian society as they face death with their families and loved ones. They are trying to come to grips with their beliefs about God.

They have been taught that God gives only good, but now all of a sudden here comes something bad. And how do you pray to God to take away the pain, they wonder, when maybe God gave them the pain? These are questions in the hearts of people like your friend.

At times, we try to give comfort to others but say just the wrong thing: "Your child is now in heaven, and he is much happier there" or "God gave you this cross to bear because you were strong enough to bear it." "Oh, that I had been weaker," the friend cries.

Nothing can heal your friend's grief but time. Man grapples with the meaning of life, and eventually he comes to certain terms with it.

Man grapples with the meaning of life, and eventually he comes to certain terms with it.

THE REAL TRUTH

I've been on the path of ECK for almost a year and a half. If the teachings really work, how come I can't Soul Travel, even after so many months of trying? Please give me some proof that Eckankar is the right path to follow. I want to know truth.

It is possible that Eckankar is not for you. That is for you to decide. Whatever path you choose, consider carefully: Do you want truth on your terms?

Truth never is what people would expect. It challenges, catches off guard, or gets the seeker leaning the other way. I hope you see what I'm driving at here. There is *belief* in ECK. That leads to *experiences,* which brings *awareness.*

To return to the point made earlier: One who expects truth to come on his terms will never find it at all. That's the cause of dissatisfaction. Open your heart so that you may find love. It's worth more than all the experiences put together. But first you must find humility, for truth won't enter an impure heart.

Growth takes time. The earth can move an inch a year a mile under the ground, and nobody cares. But when it jolts twenty feet in a minute, that's a destructive earthquake.

Growth takes time, and we are going along at a fast clip. Behind all the outer trappings, the spiritual tests go on.

When love enters the heart, no room is left for fear or doubt. But this change in heart takes time and resists force in any way.

AN ORDERLY LIFE

I have come to the realization that I am responsible for my own spiritual unfoldment, and I feel uncomfortable depending on the Mahanta to take care of me. I do feel I have guidance, but I don't understand truly what the Mahanta is. Should I stay on the path of ECK?

I greatly appreciate your sincere questions and will not try to make up your mind for you.

It's true that one can arrive at an awareness of the presence of God every moment. A mistake is to withdraw from life to sit in contemplation all day, convincing ourselves it's done because of a great love for God, when really we're hiding from the lessons of living. A God-Realized person, if you're looking for a rule of thumb, has his physical life, as well as spiritual, in order. He earns his keep.

The only purpose of the outer teachings of Eckankar is to lead you, in the most direct way, to the inner worlds. That's the source of personal

When love enters the heart, no room is left for fear or doubt. But this change in heart takes time and resists force in any way.

Mastership that develops through the actual experience of the Sound and Light of God.

A common reason for failure with the spiritual works is a lack of discipline in the practice of the Spiritual Exercises of ECK. They must be done as stated, and regularly. Experiment occasionally with them; after all, they are *creative* techniques.

SELF-DISCIPLINE

Can you help me with my self-discipline?

Each one of us in the lower worlds is struggling with self-discipline. We find it in everything we do, in our job or at home. It means, Can I get up in the morning on time? We have all these little things in our lives which are teaching us greater discipline.

I can't give you self-discipline, motivation, or even spirituality. In fact I can't give you anything. All I can do is help you in your own efforts. First of all, you have to figure out what your goal is.

Your goal can be anything, but it should be God-Realization.

Your goal can be anything, but it should be God-Realization. Not in the limited sense we've understood in orthodox religions, but in the sense of becoming one with Divine Spirit. Once we set that as our goal, then it depends on how fervently we want it.

Every so often you'll see a high-school student going down the street with a basketball in hand. Everywhere he goes he's got his basketball. He dribbles here, he dribbles there. It looks like the guy's lost his mind, but it's that kind of devotion that's needed to get to a goal. He wants to be the best player.

What are you really looking for? What are you expecting the ECK to do for you, and how do you expect to be different?

Often we want enlightenment because the life we

have today is hard. We have pains, aging starts catching up with us, the body won't run like it used to. But the true reason for spiritual enlightenment is not to escape this life but to learn how to live it richly, to enjoy it.

It's up to us to put the effort into it, to develop the self-discipline to practice the spiritual exercises.

HOW BADLY DO YOU WANT GOD?

When I have doubts about the path of ECK, I lose the motivation to do my spiritual exercises. I am not sure about the role of Eckankar in my life.

The path of ECK is actually for those who want to reach the God Consciousness in a certain, direct line. There are many paths to God, and I feel everyone should have the choice of his own religious way without fear from any outside source.

Motivation for doing the spiritual exercises is all part of our self-discipline. There is really very little that another can do to help us with that. It is a measure of how badly we want something and what we are willing to do to earn it. No one else can make that decision for another.

There are many paths to God, and I feel everyone should have the choice of his own religious way without fear from any outside source.

I believe I have reached a very high initiation inwardly, although I have not received any outer initiations. I had an experience where I saw God. Can you confirm this, please?

Though the experience you had was of a certain kind, it was not the ultimate experience of God. There are many tests initiated by the negative force, as the servant of God. They are designed to mislead any individual on the path to God.

*When one
has earned
true Self-
and God-
Realization,
he must first
have received
a number of
initiations on
the physical.*

When one has earned true Self- and God-Realization, he must first have received a number of initiations on the physical. The ECK Masters bring a person along slowly to insure that he gets every opportunity to absorb the increasingly greater Sound Current and not go out of balance.

Thus the first eight initiations are given by the Living ECK Master on the physical plane, after a good many years between each initiation. The reason is to see what the individual does at that level before he is allowed entrance into the next plane.

Anyone who has earned God-Realization is self-sufficient and has his life in order in every degree. A yardstick for the God-Realized individual is that he is able to pay his own way in society and take care of himself.

Out of Control

Lately I've hardly been able to cope with my out-of-control emotions. I've always been tormented by emotional storms—depression, tears, fierce anger, strong anxieties. I've been contacted inwardly by something called the Irona Group, who seem to be guiding me along a specific path of development. But my latest outbreak of emotional distress coincided with the Irona Group's trying to give me direct mental contact with an entity. I'm asking for your help to understand this.

You asked for help to contain the emotional storms that have affected you from an early age. Some of the things I will suggest you may have tried and may sound elementary, but look over them again.

The Irona Group says they made contact with you after you suffered an injury or blow at the age of eight. It might be useful to find a good chiropractor with holistic training. A routine X ray could pinpoint health problems caused by impaired nerves. Not every chiropractor will do, only one who is comfortable with the latest scientific instruments and has a knowledge of related fields, such as acupuncture. That combination, or something on that order, is hard to find. He or she should also know nutrition.

You, in the highest state of consciousness, are Soul; and It rebels at the control that the Irona Group is hoping to impose on you. The Higher Self is like a teen who rebels when his parents want to make him live their values, when all he wants is freedom to live and think for himself: hence, the emotional distress.

So my suggestion is for you to first make sure your physical health is in order. Automatic handwriting is the means for Irona to control you, which is all right if you want that.

See if you can get help from your dreams.

FINDING HEAVEN ANYWHERE

Recently while walking the hills and talking with you, the Mahanta, I realized I was being limited by life within the society of Eckankar. I could no longer accept the idea of initiation levels. I love the ECK, but I ask your blessing in stepping away from the outer path.

I appreciate your courtesy and thoughtfulness in sending your recent note. You, of course, have the freedom to follow the call of Soul to your destination.

A thought occurs to me that Soul in the lower worlds is always bounded on all sides. No matter where we go or what we do, things are so created that

You, of course, have the freedom to follow the call of Soul to your destination.

we always bump into a wall somewhere. Sometimes it's our own wall, other times it is someone else's. No matter what, what matters is not the wall, but what we do about it.

Having passed one wall, we meet another. We exercise our full powers of creativity and get around that one too. The experience leaves us always a little more capable spiritually than before.

Limits, inner and outer, bound Soul in the lower worlds, so It finally learns to rise above them. In doing so, It can find heaven in hell; or anywhere else, for that matter.

Having passed one wall, we meet another. We exercise our full powers of creativity and get around that one too.

MORE THAN PAT ANSWERS

Having been active in Eckankar for the past six years of my life, it hurts me to have to express some real doubts and concerns about the path. Can you understand that I want truth and not pat answers?

Your questions about truth are sincere, so I will try to give you an idea of what to look for—and without pat answers, for there are none.

To review your position, it seems you want truth to fall in line with your previous ideas of what it should be. For instance, when outer evidence conflicts with what you expected to find, you are ready to discount the whole experience of illusion as a blind trail.

Maybe I'm being too general for you to catch the image I'm trying to get across to you: real truth will always be other than what you think it is; otherwise wouldn't you have it and know it? Since you know you do not have truth, it must be other than what you think it is. What does this mean?

Unless you give up old ideas of what you expect truth to be, it will always elude you. It is a principle in ECK that one must give up the dear values again and again if the veil hiding God is to be pierced. When one reaches Self-Realization, he finds the world that he's been so comfortable in (in an unsettled way) is really at a right angle to truth. And the same conventional truth seen from the vantage point of God-Realization is 180 degrees off the mark.

Now all this philosophy won't help you, nor will the reading of any book, nor the practice of any spiritual exercise, unless the desire for truth and God is absolutely pure. Have you been misled in the past in your search? Hasn't everybody? That is the nature of this life experience, which is educational for Soul.

The outer writings serve only one purpose in their lack of perfection, since perfection is not in an imperfect world: to show Soul the inner path of ECK. No one can find the Sound and Light of God by memorizing a book. The outer works can only inspire the individual to exert himself to meet the Mahanta on the inner planes. This is not really so difficult, because others are doing it.

The outer works can only inspire the individual to exert himself to meet the Mahanta on the inner planes.

I've found it a waste of time to convince anyone to stay on a job, or in ECK, in the face of serious doubts. If the individual is inclined to leave, he should. Unless he does, he is not following his inner guidance. Some people learn better in other places. Go into contemplation to see if you are one.

FEELING TRAPPED

I'm doing my daily spiritual exercises from a sense of duty rather than love and not doing them regularly. Am I losing my faith, and how do I overcome this inner barrier?

It would be easy to beg off the question with "Don't worry; life will teach you better."

You are at one of life's many crossroads which cause these feelings of doubt about your faith in ECK. But you can safely pass through this cycle by keeping your heart open to love.

Each life cycle has a growth and a fulfillment stage. We switch back and forth between them.

Each life cycle has a growth and a fulfillment stage. We switch back and forth between them. The growth phase begins with a restless feeling that urges us into a new and greater opportunity, but fear holds us back. Finally, the need for growth outweighs the fear, so perhaps we risk taking a new job, enter a relationship, or return to school to improve our skills.

The growth phase then moves on to the fulfillment stage. Here, we master the new routines that come with change and plunge into the options of our unexplored life. All our attention is upon the challenges and rewards before us.

However, the old restlessness will return. It's nothing to worry about, though. It simply means that Soul is ready to embark upon a fresh adventure of growth and fulfillment.

The company of others on the path of ECK will help you move gracefully from the state of growth to fulfillment. This community will pass along the love and support of the Mahanta whenever your fears try to shut him out.

How do you overcome the inner barrier of doubt and fear?

Put your heart into every new venture, for the Mahanta has led you through a gateway of opportunity to help you reach a higher level of ability, love, and compassion.

You also need to address the habit of thinking so much about yourself. Remember the goal: becoming a Co-worker with God. It includes seeing the good qualities in others as well as yourself.

IS THE IMAGINATION ALWAYS HELPFUL?

When I try to do a spiritual exercise and travel out of my body, my imagination always brings in unexpected things. For example if I am in a forest on the inner planes and the tree leaves remind me of eucalyptus, immediately my imagination puts me in a eucalyptus grove. Is this helpful or should I try to control the experience more?

The only way you can tell if it's helpful is to ask, What effect is it having on me? Is it something beneficial that gives me insight?

Sometimes it's not important that you end up at a place you wanted to go but merely the fact that you end up someplace. The next part of learning comes in trying to figure out where it is. An easy answer, whether it's in healing or Soul Travel, isn't always the best because it overlooks the whole purpose of the experience, which is for learning.

As long as it's a positive experience, go with it. You may not always know where you are. If you feel bad when you come back, you know right away that it wasn't good. I wouldn't worry about it; all you're doing is getting experience, and that's fine.

An easy answer, whether it's in healing or Soul Travel, isn't always the best because it overlooks the whole purpose of the experience, which is for learning.

CENSOR

How does the censor work in our dreams and in our daily lives?

A dream usually applies very directly to what's happening in your outer life, often something right at the moment. But the dream comes through disguised because it would shock us.

Divine Spirit is trying to get a message through to the lower bodies to give us a hint of how we should change our lives a little bit. But the mind says, "No. If we let that message come straight through from the chief, it would be too much for them down here. We'll reword it a little." So by the time it gets down to the physical consciousness, you can't figure out exactly what it's supposed to say.

Change usually comes gradually. It's not often an earthshaking thing like, Go out and start your own business now. And you wonder, *How will I pay my rent on the thirtieth?* Whatever you're doing right now is just right for you. When there's a change to come, it can come gradually.

Soul tries to make this gradual change but by the time the censor finishes with the information, it's diluted so you can't make heads or tails of which direction to take.

Just remember, the inner life is directly related to the outer. If you get help in the dream state, it generally applies to your immediate outer life, what you're doing right here and now. It will also put you in positions to grow in understanding.

CAVE OF PURIFICATION

I've heard about a place in the inner worlds where people go to burn off karma. It's called the cave of purification. What exactly is it? Is it real?

This is an actual location on a number of planes. Its purpose is to provide a place for a rapid burn-off of karma. The cave on the Astral Plane, the plane of emotions, is in a mountainous area.

The mouth of the cave is tall enough to allow for

Divine Spirit is trying to get a message through to the lower bodies to give us a hint of how we should change our lives a little bit.

twice the height of an average-size man. There is a huge boulder to the right of the entrance as you face the cave. A smaller rock, waist high, is on the left as you approach.

The Mahanta may bring an intiate there in the dream state. In this cave a brilliant white light burns away useless karmic burdens. The fire is white, but the flames throw no heat in the usual way. It is a fire that burns the atoms in one clean.

Sometime after this rite of purification, the individual is cleared to pass into the next plane, the Causal Plane.

CALLING FOR HELP

If you're going through an unpleasant experience in the dream state which you determine is a spiritual test, and you call on the Inner Master for help, at that moment have you passed the test or failed it?

Every answer is within your grasp, some are very close to you.

You've remembered to ask, and that is an important step because you've remembered the Inner Master. Every answer is within your grasp, some are very close to you.

When you're wandering around the lower worlds, it's possible for those beings Paul Twitchell, the modern-day founder of Eckankar, called the Time Makers to cloud your memory. They can wash your memory so that you forget there is help available simply by calling for it.

But if you have one little thought stuck away that reminds you that help is there if you ask, then you'll find another thought will come: how to extricate yourself from the situation. You'll remember the laws of the inner worlds that you may have forgotten. You'll remember, As Soul, I am free!

SOUL'S GOAL

What is the ultimate goal of Soul?

Here is a brief review of the final goal of Soul: It gathers an education in the lower worlds so that It can become a true citizen in the spiritual community. This is what we call a Co-worker with God.

The relationship between parent and child in the worlds of matter is based on this spiritual design. The parent is the vehicle for the child's entrance into the world and is responsible for his education. The child must, between birth and the age of perhaps eighteen, learn all the dos and don'ts of his culture. The significant fact underlying the parent-child relationship is that there is more freedom for the child as he gets older and assumes more responsibility. The parent has failed his duties if the child reaches legal age and is unfit to take his place in the world.

The path of Eckankar encourages the freedom and responsibility of Soul. After all, that is Its birthright.

The path of Eckankar encourages the freedom and responsibility of Soul. After all, that is Its birthright.

Every Soul is a spark of God. The child learns by making errors, but the wise parent must let the child learn for himself, giving guidance when it is necessary.

Different spiritual exercises are given in the Eckankar books, especially *The Spiritual Exercises of ECK*. Simply try them and see if they work.

9
SPIRITUAL EXERCISES

What is the purpose of Eckankar's spiritual exercises? Will they take me where I want to go spiritually?

The whole focus of Eckankar is direct experience of the Light and Sound of God. This can come through practice of the Spiritual Exercises of ECK.

Different spiritual exercises are given in the Eckankar books, especially *The Spiritual Exercises of ECK.* Simply try them, and see if they work. Don't push yourself, though. There's no reason to.

If you are successful with the spiritual exercises, you ought to become aware of either the Light or Sound of God. You may also meet the Inner Master, the Mahanta, who always awaits the individual who is sincere in seeking truth.

Some people have quite an active inner life and travel widely in the inner worlds; others are quite content to let Divine Spirit guide them indirectly in their daily lives. Let any teaching you are studying fit you instead of trying to adapt to something that is not comfortable.

Take your whole lifetime to make up your mind if you want. After all, it is your life.

The whole focus of Eckankar is direct experience of the Light and Sound of God.

Experimenting

How can I get the most out of my spiritual exercises? What should I be learning from them?

If you eat the same food every day for two weeks, it can get pretty dull. You may enjoy it the first day, and the second day is all right. But by the second week, you're tired of it. So you experiment; you experiment with something new.

It's the same with the spiritual exercises. You experiment with them; you try new things. You're in your own God Worlds. I've gone to different extremes with the exercises, trying very complicated ones I developed for myself, dropping them when they didn't work anymore.

Are we learning something new every day from what we're doing?

It's like a vein of gold running through a mountain. You're on it for a while, then the vein runs out and you have to scout around and find another one.

Are we learning something new every day from what we're doing? Are we getting insight and help from the inner? This is what we ought to be working for.

How can we face life as we find it? The key is always through the Spiritual Exercises of ECK.

Two Techniques

I have tried diligently to do my spiritual exercises but have not made the progress I hoped for. When I mentioned to a friend that my exercises last from two to two and a half hours with spotty results, she advised me to write you.

Two and a half hours is too long for the spiritual exercises. It is understandable to try harder when there is no apparent success, but the door of Soul opens inwardly. No amount of pushing from the wrong side will open it. Twenty minutes to half an hour is the limit of time to spend with the spiritual exercises during one sitting.

Alternate these two techniques:

1. Count backward slowly from ten to one, then picture yourself standing alongside your resting physical body. Do this for a few weeks. You may also recite the alphabet backward from *J* to *A*.

2. The second method is done when you've finished contemplation and are getting ready for bed. Say inwardly to the Mahanta, who is also the Dream Master, "I give you permission to take me into the Far Country, to the place that is right for me now." Then go to sleep without giving the thought command another bit of attention. The command unlocks the unconscious so the experiences of Soul can be retained by the human mind.

Practice these two methods for a month, with a notebook within easy reach to make notes.

Experiences of the Higher Planes

Sometimes the Sound and Light of God come to me before I can even start a spiritual exercise. The Light comes in huge waves, the Sound is loud and in the distance. Why does this happen?

The experiences are often very vivid when we first begin practicing the Spiritual Exercises of ECK. As we go into the subtler regions beyond the Causal Plane, they become less and less vivid. That's when you find the experiences with the Sound and Light are fewer and farther between.

When that happens, what keeps a person going?

The experiences are often very vivid when we first begin practicing the Spiritual Exercises of ECK.

That's when they must work toward self-mastery and begin carrying this Sound and Light of God, that they may no longer hear or see, out into the world.

Self-mastery is what the spiritual life is all about.

Self-mastery is what the spiritual life is all about.

OUT OF THE BODY

A few minutes after I start to contemplate, with my attention fixed on my Spiritual Eye, I feel a slight pressure inside my forehead. Is this a step toward an out-of-body experience, or Soul Travel?

It's Soul getting ready to go out of the body through the Third Eye, which is located just above and a little behind the space between the eyebrows.

SEEING AN INNER EYE

I have been visited several times by an eye which appears on my inner screen. It always brings a feeling of love. What is it?

The single eye you see means your final destiny is complete service and devotion to God. Soul is actually chosen by God before It becomes aware that It is one of the chosen ones.

Usually, people who see the eye miss the desertlike world upon which they stand while viewing it. This means that all substance and life for Soul is beyond the sandy wastes of the lower worlds. The only goal for such a one as you is God, the Ocean of Love and Mercy.

CHANGING THE WAY YOU CONTEMPLATE

Are there times when it is best not to do a spiritual exercise? When the negative energies in my life become overwhelming, I try to stop what I am doing and do a short spiritual exercise. But I wonder whether there are times when it would be better to just wait out the period of difficulty.

Keep doing the spiritual exercises, but do them in a different way.

People often get more intense with their spiritual exercises when things appear to go wrong. Why? Perhaps because they want to force something in their life to go where *they* feel it ought to go. Or, the going is tougher than they expected.

Do a spiritual exercise anyway when all goes wrong. However, do it with a new thought in mind. Say to the Mahanta, "What is thy will?" Then chant a sacred word, such as the name for God, HU. Put your full attention on the problem, for the Mahanta will show you how you can grow spiritually by meeting the problem.

HU opens your heart to God, the ECK, and the Mahanta. In other words, it opens you to God's sweet love.

HU opens your heart to God, the ECK, and the Mahanta.

THREE INNER SOUNDS

I am intrigued by, but don't quite understand, the significance of this: I constantly hear three separate sounds of ECK anytime I give my attention to them when in a quiet place.

You are operating in the higher planes where Soul can listen to melodies from several sources at once.

Examples of the higher sounds that one might hear include the high whistle that is like a teakettle in the kitchen signaling that the water is boiling. Another sound, similar to it but still higher in pitch, is a series of intermittent beeps, rather than the steady, continuous whistle of the former. A third sound is sometimes heard in conjunction with the first two: running water.

Of course, these are only examples of the various combinations that can be heard. Any combination of the Audible Life Stream melodies may come to one who does the Spiritual Exercises of ECK with love.

The sound of running water in the example above is the anchor for the other two sounds, the whistle and the beep. One of the three sounds you hear is likewise the anchor which tethers Soul close enough to the body for the mind to recall the music from the upper planes.

Soul, in the higher viewpoint, has the advantage of simultaneously looking at several of the planes at once, to collect the knowledge and wisdom that is available to It. Keep up the spiritual exercises, for they are the door to the Ocean of Love and Mercy.

Any combination of the Audible Life Stream melodies may come to one who does the Spiritual Exercises of ECK with love.

CURTAIN OF MEMORY

I often lose conscious awareness during the spiritual exercises. One moment I am chanting, and the next thing I know, twenty minutes have passed. What has happened during this time?

This is not at all unusual. The Inner Master has simply pulled the curtain on your memory. Divine Spirit, the ECK, takes us into full consciousness at our own pace. That's why Eckankar is an individual path to God.

As you develop spiritual stamina, your memory will retain bits and pieces of your inner experience. What is important, however, is to continue faithfully with the spiritual exercises.

Contemplation Time

Do you have any suggestions on how to start good patterns for doing spiritual exercises? I set a time, then something else to do always comes up instead. When I change the time to do them, it feels like the pattern gets goofed up.

It's better to do the spiritual exercises at different times than not do them at all.

You can also try choosing a time when other things might not interfere, like right before bedtime.

As you practice the spiritual exercises, pretty soon you will be able to tune in to the Holy Spirit, the ECK, anywhere, no matter what time it is. You will be able to do it easily, no matter where you are.

In contemplation, when I place my attention on my Third Eye, above and between my eyebrows, it always begins to sway and move around. This makes me yawn and disturbs my spiritual exercise. Do you have any suggestions?

The mind gets bored fast. So if it makes you yawn when you place your attention on the Third Eye, then put your attention on your crown chakra instead. That's at the top of your head. That spiritual center is actually the easiest place to succeed at Soul Travel.

Spiritual Vitamins

I don't feel anything when I chant my secret word, my personal mantra. Could I be doing something wrong? How does Soul link up with the ECK through mantras?

The personal mantra has no power but by the Mahanta. The secret word fits the individual's rate

As you practice the spiritual exercises, pretty soon you will be able to tune in to the Holy Spirit, the ECK, anywhere.

of vibration and is the tuning fork that puts him in tune. The ECK is one and the same, but each Soul is at a different level of consciousness. The word attunes one to the ECK.

Please do not become discouraged by your apparent inability to have any experiences during contemplation. The secret word is like a spiritual vitamin that builds one's inner strength over a certain length of time. Deep changes occur in you when you chant your word. Karma is dissolved from the lower bodies until the weight on Soul is lightened.

Within twelve months, you should find yourself suddenly in a new and joyful inner state that will prove to you once and for all that you are Soul, a spark of God.

How's Your Desire for God?

Desire for God must become an all-consuming fire for Soul, and not just an avocation.

I'm not a member of Eckankar, but I am sincerely endeavoring to have some of the experiences that followers of Eckankar seem to have. Is it possible that my failures are due to Soul simply being not yet ready to receive the ECK? Am I wasting my time?

Desire for God must become an all-consuming fire for Soul, and not just an avocation. Only a single-minded effort to reach the Light and Sound of ECK will bring success. You must want to learn the ways of Divine Spirit as much as a drowning man craves air. Yet this must be an inner drive that gives purpose and balance to the outer life. Avoid austerities and love the Spirit of God within you.

Ignoring Guidance

If someone slacks off on their spiritual exercises for a period of time, does he or she still have the guidance of the Mahanta? Can one still be in touch with the ECK at this time?

Let me answer you like this: One day in late spring I took a walk near a pond. The sun was very hot. On the edge of the grass by the water stood a duck. Under her were three ducklings using her for a sunscreen.

Someone on the path of ECK who neglects the spiritual exercises is like a duckling who leaves the protection of its mother. He is ignoring the guidance of the Master. His contact with the Light and Sound of ECK will only be a small part of what it was before.

When the sun of karma gets too hot for comfort, like the duckling, he can run back to his sunscreen— the Mahanta. The run back is the spiritual exercise.

Continue with the Spiritual Exercises of ECK. It is only an illusion from one of the mental passions that convinces us we have learned all there is to know. When we give up and let go, then we slip into the dawn of a new spiritual day. As surely as the night, the dawn appears. That is true in all things. There is always one more step that you can take.

It is only an illusion from one of the mental passions that convinces us we have learned all there is to know.

DIRECT INFORMATION

In my spiritual exercises, I get direct information about what's needed in the moment. But these aren't grand inner experiences. Is this just a passing phase? Is there a technique I could do to be a more conscious explorer of the Far Country?

There is a way to be more aware of your travels in the higher worlds. You must train your mind to recall details. This means developing the power of your imagination, which is a lot harder than it sounds, but there is an enjoyable way to go about it.

Do you play golf? Let's say you have trouble with a slice when you tee off. You can work out that problem both here in the physical world and on the inner planes.

Get a book by a golf pro that shows ways to correct a slice. Study the exact methods given. Then, when you lie down for the night or while at rest some other time, imagine yourself on a golf course. Now practice the expert's advice—all in your imagination. Address the ball, hit it in the proper way, and watch it fly straight down the fairway. Do this again and again. Pay attention to your grip, your stance, and the position of your arms and head.

If you are a golfer, you'll like this exercise. It works with any sport.

Your game will improve, but more important, you'll soon find it easier to recall your journeys into the higher worlds of God.

The daily exercise of twenty or thirty minutes gives a better focus and a deeper strength to your life.

LIVING SPIRITUAL EXERCISE

At a recent seminar, you talked about being a living spiritual exercise. Does that mean I don't have to do my spiritual exercises for thirty minutes a day?

The daily exercise of twenty or thirty minutes gives a better focus and a deeper strength to your life. It is what lets you be a living spiritual exercise the whole day long.

FALLING ASLEEP

Why can't I stay awake during the spiritual exercises? I always seem to fall asleep, and I feel like I'm missing something.

Do not be overly concerned by falling asleep during the spiritual exercises. Sometimes this is the only way Divine Spirit can work with us at first.

This is also true when we don't remember our dream state.

You can finish the Spiritual Exercises of ECK in the evening before bedtime, then carry a light sort of contemplation to bed with you. This is done simply by lying down at night to go to sleep and saying something like this: "Please, Mahanta, take me to the place in the heavenly worlds that is suitable for me tonight. I place all my love and confidence in your decision."

Then erase the entire resolution from your mind. Go to sleep in a normal manner without concern whether or not anything will happen. Take your time, and don't hurry.

FREE SPIRIT

I don't know the purpose of the spiritual exercises. Now that I am on the path of ECK, I have a hard time feeling like I fit in. As I was growing up, my father believed I could find my own religion when I was ready. He never explained anything in terms of God; it was always in terms of nature. Where am I?

I much appreciate your letter asking for help to understand your spiritual place in life. By upbringing and training you are a "free child." Your methods of contemplation are simple and direct, and should be upon some aspect of nature. The mental route is not for you, because you instinctively feel the pulse of life by just being who you are.

There is room for you to express how you'd like to live in ECK, and it may be quite different from what others on the path of ECK find comfortable.

Do not be overly concerned by falling asleep during the spiritual exercises. Sometimes this is the only way Divine Spirit can work with us at first.

The spiritual exercises are to open you to divine love. You are able to design your own exercises through your love and respect for the things of nature. Your path to love, wisdom, and power is unique, but under the surface, so is everyone's.

CHARGED WORDS

Can spiritually charged words such as HU *be overused, as were* God *and* abracadabra? *And, is it OK to change the inflection, tone, or meaning of such words in songs, jokes, or conversation?*

God and *abracadabra* lost their meaning when people lost the Living Word. The Sound Current was beyond their reach, and the priests could not lead them to It. Perhaps it was frustration with a dead religion that first led people to take the holy names of God in vain.

One who communicates daily with the Word of God, the ECK, can only speak words of joy and reverence.

One who communicates daily with the Word of God, the ECK, can only speak words of joy and reverence. The Sound and Light are his heartbeat and breath, his golden love. How can he then but love God—and himself? Pure and holy songs spring from a pure and golden heart.

This also answers your second question.

TAKING A BREAK

This seems to me to be one of the most difficult years in my life, not only physically but spiritually. I had a dream about a young girl from India who had thin slats for legs. I was trying to teach her to dance. What does this mean?

The dream was to confirm for you that the approach of the Eastern religions (the young Indian girl) is stilted (she had thin slats for legs). It's much more difficult to learn the rhythm of dancing on such legs. The dream implies the need to learn the rhythm of life.

For a month, just forget about doing the formal ECK spiritual exercises. You will still have my protection. Use that month to see how the ECK is revealing Itself to you through the words and actions of other people.

Watch both for things that are harmonious to you but also things that upset you. Try to be very honest now. After each experience, ask yourself, Am I changed even a little? If so, how?

The teachings must fit your spiritual needs. Other people have different needs, so their inner guidance for living does not necessarily apply to you. For some people, it's also a spiritual exercise to serve their family and enjoy the happiness that their attention and love gives to their loved ones.

After each experience, ask yourself, Am I changed even a little? If so, how?

There are as many ways to communicate with the ECK (meaning, to do the spiritual exercises) as there are people. Do what seems natural and good to you. Listen to your inner guidance in this regard, and don't let anyone make you feel guilty about the way you choose to return to God.

Also, if you feel that Eckankar is not going in your direction anymore, please feel free to leave it with my blessings. You, and everyone, have the right to choose your own direction in life. That is your spiritual right.

MEDITATION

My husband began meditation a short time ago and has changed considerably. He used to be a good doctor but has stopped that. He is so silent now. He's decided that money is no good; but how can we survive without it? We have four children. What can I do?

I am not able to interfere in family matters. But I can give you an understanding into meditation, which induces lethargy.

Many do not know the act of leaving their loved ones to follow God is not necessary.

Many do not know the act of leaving their loved ones to follow God is not necessary. We must accept responsibility first for the obligations that we have taken on in this life. Even family men have become saints in that they found the source of all life—the Sound and Light of Divine Spirit through the Spiritual Exercises of ECK.

I also have a family to care for. Although it would be much simpler to run away from my duties, I know that the Divine Essence is working through my daily life and family to give me what I need to unfold spiritually.

The monks who hide from life are mistaken that God loves them more for giving up their duties. There is nothing evil about money nor the ability to pay one's way in this world. The spiritual law is that everything must be paid for in the true coin. Eckankar is not a spiritual welfare program.

You may turn the matter over to Divine Spirit for It to handle however It may choose, and in Its own time. The love of the Holy Spirit is always with you.

AM I DOING SOMETHING WRONG?

I've been on the path of ECK for twelve years and haven't been able to recognize any spiritual experiences. Am I doing something wrong?

The first natural question one has when memory of the spiritual exercises is not forthcoming is that perhaps there is something wrong. Please be assured that the Master is always with you. The meetings with the Mahanta are constant, whether one remembers them or not. The Light and Sound that come to one on the inner levels translate to service of love to others in the outer life during waking hours.

The whole key to the works of Eckankar is the spiritual exercises. What is often missing during the practice of these exercises, if they are done daily, is love or good feeling in the heart center. The contemplative exercises will not work unless one practices them with love and goodwill.

Often it helps to think of something happy from years ago, or someone today who has brought you a feeling of warmth. Then if you can carry this feeling of upliftment with you into contemplation, you stand a better chance of success.

Not all who are on the path of ECK are aware of Divine Spirit coming to them through the Light and Sound, but they see Its influence in their daily lives. This help comes only after we have tried to solve a problem ourselves, as if the solution depended completely upon us. Then we often get a little help for the problem to come into resolution.

I've put a lot of attention on Soul Travel as the natural way for expansion of consciousness and travel into the spiritual worlds of God. This was needed by many. Soul Travel is often missed by a person who is not aware of a rushing movement out of the body; therefore, he is satisfied to call his experience a vivid dream, when it was really Soul Travel.

The Holy Spirit, the ECK, actually fills all our nooks and crannies with Itself. We feel so comfortable with life as it is—and rightfully so—that we

The contemplative exercises will not work unless one practices them with love and goodwill.

must be reminded to review what uncertainty life was before ECK.

Divine Spirit is indeed in our innermost being. Therefore, we are instruments of love. This is what attracts people to us and makes us natural leaders. So even if you are not yet aware of Soul Travel, or the Sound and Light, the ECK is coming through you all the time.

You are serving It by your very being.

Divine Spirit is indeed in our innermost being. Therefore, we are instruments of love.

Do We Have Inner Protection?

I am disturbed by a figure I see in contemplation that seems to be attacking me.

Conflicts take place on the inner and outer planes, but the people who are the main characters in the play never suspect that the whole world of ECK is watching every gesture with great interest.

The actors think they are performing in their attics, judging by some of the things they say and do. But it's all done onstage, never behind the scenes as they imagine.

The pain is always greatest when we find that the person who is trying to harm us is someone we entrust our lives to. The person you saw during contemplation thinks he is the actor hidden in his own attic where nobody can see him. But we all know his lines.

It depends on whether he is going the way of love or power. This choice is his, the free will that is the whole measure of ECK.

Your inner travels will mostly be what they appear to be, but it pays to be skeptical if someone claims to be even the Master. Does his visit leave you feeling up or on edge? The "up" feeling is the Mahanta.

WHO IS THIS MASTER?

While doing a spiritual exercise, a picture flashed before my Spiritual Eye. It was a man in a white robe, with a healthy head of black, curly hair and a long beard. Who is this Master?

Zadok, who served as the Living ECK Master during the time of Jesus, is often seen like this. (Sometimes differently, though.)

SOUND ALL THE TIME

Why do I hear the Sound Current constantly in Its many aspects? A friend says she hears It only in contemplation.

I wish everyone had your ability to hear the ECK so clearly, but the Mahanta realizes that for some the Sound would be a distraction.

There are cases of people in business who simply could not function at their jobs because the Holy Music of God drowned out conversations needed to carry out their duties. So the Mahanta shut down the Sound Current (just the audible aspect of It).

You hear the Sound all the time because of your ability to incorporate It into the activities of your daily life. You are most fortunate.

You hear the Sound all the time because of your ability to incorporate It into the activities of your daily life. You are most fortunate.

ENHANCING OUR OWN EFFORTS

I've been doing the spiritual exercises for a few months, but my spouse says I'm not any easier to get along with. Why aren't they working better? Should I be doing them longer or more often?

The Spiritual Exercises of ECK open us to be a

vehicle for Divine Spirit. We develop harmony and common sense in our dealings with others. The greatest challenge for us to learn is how to work with the spiritual insight and incorporate it into our daily lives.

The path of Eckankar merely enhances our own efforts toward Self- and God-Realization as we come to trust the guidance that comes from the inner planes. We keep on living our lives, paying our own way. Outwardly, an observer may see no change in us. The difference is that now we begin to reflect the subtle nudges of ECK in our decisions and plans.

The spiritual exercises are like physical exercises. Don't run a mile the first time out jogging. Go slowly. Build up stamina.

The spiritual exercises are like physical exercises. Don't run a mile the first time out jogging. Go slowly. Build up stamina. Otherwise you burn out and cause a lot of needless personal stress. Find the balance. You have common sense about this.

WHAT'S THE CAUSE?

Anytime I start doing the contemplative exercises, I always begin to have a lot of personal problems. The problems make me afraid to resume the exercises. I have gone through a divorce, I filed for bankruptcy, and I've lost my job and can't get a new one. I feel like I need to do the techniques but fear the consequences.

I can understand your reluctance to do the contemplative exercises when on the surface they appear to be the cause of your rash of troubles. So you feel yourself torn in two directions at once: to do the Spiritual Exercises of ECK, or not.

You must remember that life can only return to us what we've sent out previously. When so many things go wrong in our lives, we sure don't like to think ourselves responsible. But life returns our former deeds to us. It is the most difficult thing on earth to own up to our responsibility. Perhaps that's why so few people do.

The spiritual exercises, as you can see from your own experiences, have a definite power to set things into motion. All we're ever doing is facing ourselves. And each person has his unique experiences in ECK, for It will only try to clear away the problems that an individual has been carrying along with him, like unpaid bank charges. For once one's individual karmic debt begins to clear up, he suddenly finds that life becomes easier, more forgiving, and a greater pleasure to live.

So should you start up with the spiritual exercises again? You'll have to go into contemplation, perhaps each day over a period of several weeks or months, and decide for yourself with the help of the Mahanta, the Inner Master. At all times, in all ways, I am with you spiritually.

The spiritual exercises, as you can see from your own experiences, have a definite power to set things into motion.

What's in Your Heart?

I often find myself using a kind of prayer to talk with the Mahanta. I speak of what's in my heart at the time, but I don't have the experiences that others have with the spiritual exercises. Am I missing the true experience of the Light and Sound?

By now you should be more aware of the love of the Mahanta in your spiritual life. Though the outer things we love are put to the trial, the Inner Master is with us at all times. Please know that your concerns are in the hands of the ECK, which is always working on behalf of your greatest good.

A spiritual exercise that may help you to open up to the Mahanta is a simple one. Every morning upon awakening, say to God, "I am a child of the ECK, and I move and have my being in the arms of Its love." Then go about your day in sweet confidence, for the presence of the Mahanta will be with you everywhere, even in the most troubling of times.

You will be a shining light to all who need help, for you are then a clear and open channel for the Sound and Light of ECK. It will gently reach out through you to bring comfort or healing of spirit to those near you who need it.

Sing quietly to the Mahanta, "I love you with all my heart. Take me home."

A spiritual exercise for bedtime that may be useful to you is the following: Sing quietly to the Mahanta, "I love you with all my heart. Take me home."

Then, with your eyes still shut, look at the screen in your inner mind and imagine it to be white. Have a movie projector set up in front of the screen and run a film of a meeting with the Mahanta. Talk with me in contemplation as you would if we were in the same room physically. Talk about those things which are a sorrow to your heart, but remember to speak also of the blessings which the ECK is giving you every day, but which are easily forgotten.

RELAXING IMAGES

Yesterday morning right after waking up, there suddenly came into clear inner view a picture of a person sitting in a rocking chair, like the one in the painting of Whistler's mother. The picture remained clear for about ten seconds, a little longer than usual, then it faded. What does this mean?

The significance of the picture with a person in the rocker is simply this: the Mahanta puts a familiar, nonthreatening image on the screen so that you could become confident in the naturalness of contact with the inner planes.

Even as the picture stayed longer than those in the past, so is the Holy Spirit, the ECK, in your consciousness for increasing periods of time. You must continue the spiritual exercises and the greater truths will be shown you in time.

CREATIVE PRINCIPLES

I've been gaining some insight recently into the reality and power of the creative imagination. There are two material things I would like to bring into my life, so I have been using those situations as test projects to focus my attention on. There is, however, another direction I want to focus on with the imaginative techniques—a more spiritual direction. I want to visit the inner planes and establish an inner life there, which I can be aware of and move about in consciously.

It was good to see that you're working on the principle of the creative imagination. All the worlds and planes do indeed lie behind the thinnest of veils. Reality is what the imagination can see as a picture fulfilled. Words are too awkward to tell of the simplicity of how this principle works.

Reality is what the imagination can see as a picture fulfilled.

Know that the inner worlds do exist. Humbly ask the Mahanta before sleep to take you to one of them. Chant HU or Z, which is my true spiritual name. Relax your anxieties and know that the Mahanta, the Inner Master, will suddenly put you into one of the locations in the Far Country when all preparations have been made.

Facing Your Doubts

I have trouble doing my spiritual exercises; part of me doubts that I am getting anywhere. Can you give me a sign that I am on the right path?

Words are such a poor way to convey truth, so I hesitate to use them, but sometimes there is no better way. The experiences of life are simply to open us to the love of God. However, without meaning to, we often take a roundabout route to it.

The reason is mainly due to our unconscious memories of past betrayals of our affections. When we finally meet the Mahanta, we're not sure about him. We hold back, not wanting to suffer pain and disillusionment again.

Our fears become so ingrained that we actually begin to draw pain and disillusionment toward us outwardly. Fear drives away love. Without love, there is no surrender of all our inner cares and worries to the Mahanta.

Soul (you, in the Higher Self, of course) wants to find divine love and serve God.

So you see, we enter a vicious cycle that seems to have no way out. I don't like to advocate blind faith to anyone, but in some cases the blind leap of faith is the only way to outrun fear and find love.

All the problems you have are really with one cause: Soul (you, in the Higher Self, of course) wants to find divine love and serve God. A short contemplation to try in order to bring love into your life is this: "I come to thee, Mahanta, and open my heart to love."

There is no force greater than love. It will begin to enter you and make those changes which are spiritually good for you.

The ECK Masters lead the inexperienced Soul to self-mastery by awakening love in one's heart.

10

PAST LIVES AND SPIRITUAL PROTECTION

I've read about miracles and have been asking for help and protection. Why don't I see results?

While it is true that some people get help from the ECK in a flashy, outward way, many people do not. What have we earned? Just asking for God's gift does not bring it. Jesus said, while offering help to the sick, "According to your faith be it unto you." According to your faith . . .

Divine Spirit opens up new opportunities, but we must take them. The ECK Masters lead the inexperienced Soul to self-mastery by awakening love in one's heart. You must make your own choices with the best information at hand. Only then can the Holy Spirit help and guide you in your decisions.

The ECK Masters lead the inexperienced Soul to self-mastery by awakening love in one's heart.

CAN YOU SEE PAST LIVES?

I would like to see my past lives. How do I go about this?

It is easiest to trace past lives through a study of your dreams.

To awaken such past-life dreams, make a note of things you greatly like or dislike. Do that also with people. Then watch your dreams. Also note if a certain country or century attracts you. There is a reason.

When we practice the Spiritual Exercises of ECK faithfully, the Inner Master will open us up to those things that are important to see concerning past lives. Most of them need not concern us. No matter what we were in the past during any other life, we are spiritually greater today.

No matter what we were in the past during any other life, we are spiritually greater today.

The wealth and position we enjoyed in past lives mean nothing unless we know how to lift ourselves from materialism into the higher worlds. This does not mean to shun the good things of this life—family, home, wealth. God loves the rich man as much as the poor. We get no special benefits if we fall for the negative tricks of asceticism or unusual austerities.

We live the spiritual life beginning where we are today. We look to see the hand of Divine Spirit guiding us toward the greater consciousness, which leads us to becoming a more direct vehicle for Spirit.

How Are You Spiritually Protected?

My husband and I feel we are under psychic attack much of the time. We took a course in another line of teaching and learned that many of our problems are caused by those outside ourselves. I thought that being a member of Eckankar protected us from this sort of thing.

I appreciated your letter about the subject of psychic attacks. One must keep in mind that earth is a training ground for Soul to open Itself as a vehicle for Divine Spirit. What then blocks Soul from instantly recognizing Itself in Self- and God-

Realization? Not yet knowing how to control the five passions of the mind (lust, anger, greed, undue attachment to material things, and vanity).

We personally are responsible for our own state of consciousness. That results in a particular series of situations in our life. As Soul unfolds toward total freedom, It understands total responsibility must be accepted for every thought and action.

Mixing two different paths splits our consciousness. We owe it to our own spiritual development to choose a path to God, whatever it is, and live it.

If psychic attacks bother us, it's because sometime in the past we have opened the door. If it's a real problem, one must seek licensed counseling.

HOW TO UNWIND YOUR KARMA

My husband left me suddenly almost five years ago, and I cannot get my life nor my finances straightened out. After reading many books I was beginning to develop psychic abilities, but then they stopped. Please check my Akashic records to see why these things are happening.

While the Akashic, or past life, records of anyone are important in determining certain causes and effects in his life, most of the problems that arise from the past cannot be solved simply by a knowledge of it. Otherwise most psychic readers who are good at reading the Akashic records would be able to help people straighten out unhappy lives at will.

But this does not happen. Somebody must have the knowledge of how to begin unwinding the intricate karma that has brought one to the present-day trouble. This is a spiritual skill that is known to very few of those who can read the past records.

We owe it to our own spiritual development to choose a path to God, whatever it is, and live it.

The Adepts in ECK have a single purpose in mind when a seeker comes to them for relief: to give that Soul the opportunity for achieving wisdom, power, and freedom, three attributes of God-Realization. This means simply that an individual learns to be like the Adepts, enjoying a 360-degree viewpoint, the center of which is a love for all living things.

He is no longer at the mercy of destiny and the blind fates, but becomes a knowing being who understands the secret laws that govern his affairs.

When one gains a degree of this love, he is himself able to restructure his life along lines that suit him. He is no longer at the mercy of destiny and the blind fates, but becomes a knowing being who understands the secret laws that govern his affairs. He is like the sailor who knows the ocean currents; he can chart a course to a destination and be quite certain of getting there in his sailboat.

Most of the cause for your present trouble is indeed from the past, but not in the desertion of your mate then or now. There is a tendency for you to lean upon others, to let them think for you. When this rubber crutch is leaned upon, it gives way and you fall down, at the mercy of every sort of misfortune that can be imagined. Therefore, the lesson that Soul must learn in this case is to find a more substantial inner support than It has in the past.

Your problems with failing finances are simply due to a lack of knowledge about the ins and outs of finance. I suggest you make an effort to learn about the financial areas that would be most helpful to you in the immediate future. If you let go and give your concerns to Divine Spirit, you will be guided to the best avenue to take next. Look over all the different ways open to you to learn about finance: local courses in the community, help from a friend who is well off in money matters, or books in the library.

There is no more magic about setting oneself up

financially than there is for an experienced cook to bake a cake. There is a recipe for success no matter what field one is in. Failure, like a fallen angel-food cake, means the cook overlooked something important in the baking process that a better cook does by second nature.

There is a recipe for success no matter what field one is in.

Too many people want to use the psychic field as a shortcut to improving their lives. They feel there is a magical route that will leapfrog them over the hardship of self-discipline. The psychic field is set in an unstable force and will fail just as a person thinks he has a certain method for predicting the future down pat.

In ECK, I want to show people how to become open channels for Divine Spirit. Remember, Soul has come into the lower worlds in many different incarnations in order to learn to be a Co-worker with God. A mechanical method of restructuring your life will fail unless there is also an upliftment in consciousness. I recommend you try the simple spiritual exercise called the Easy Way technique, given on page 150. It is one way of opening oneself to the more bountiful life of Spirit.

PERSONAL PROTECTION

I live with another person who uses drugs. How can drug abuse affect others living under the same roof, who do not share the habit, and who are not aware when this is happening?

The love and protection of the ECK are with you in all spiritual concerns. In regard to the effect that a user of recreational drugs has upon others who live with him but do not use drugs themselves, the full responsibility for any karma created by such an act is borne by the user of drugs alone. He is also held accountable if others should stumble on the path to God because of his self-indulgent appetite for drugs.

Only his own aura is pierced, but when his karmic load is increased by the Lords of Karma, naturally it will also have a secondhand effect upon all who are near to him, although he must bear his own punishments.

The answer I'm giving you here is only part of the full answer to your situation. The other part will be given by the Inner Master and may be consciously recalled upon awakening in the morning or not. Nevertheless, be assured that the Mahanta is now starting to resolve the situation for your spiritual benefit. Watch closely how Divine Spirit does this, for Its ways are beyond the ways of men.

Protection from Others

There are several means of protection that are possible to use against those who intrude into our state of being.

I have been aware that members of a religious group I used to be involved in are still trying to get me under their influence. Besides outer ways—mail and phone calls—they are appearing in my dreams. I would like to know how to protect myself from them.

There are several means of protection that are possible to use against those who intrude into our state of being. One simple method is putting a reversed mirror between yourself and the harm. This is done by imagining a mockup of a mirror that reflects back to the sender all unwanted thoughts and forces.

Another form of self-protection is to put yourself in a white circle of light. Then look out from this center at whatever is disturbing you. You may also imagine a wall that shields you from the psychic enemy.

Those are inward solutions. If you find the need, do whatever is necessary on the physical level. In case they are able to bother you physically, it may be necessary to ask for protection from the legal authorities. When the force is all subtle, consider calling competent counseling and tell them what is troubling you. Ask what, if anything, can be done for you. The local hospital ought to be able to give you the names of licensed counselors.

The Holy Spirit often works through professional medical people to help us out when we're in trouble. After all, all healing comes from Divine Spirit, no matter what It chooses as Its instrument.

FRIENDS FROM THE PAST

In my dreams, I am often with friends from the past whom I no longer see in the physical. These people had a big influence in my life at one time, but why are they in my dreams so often today?

Your question deals with the very broad sweep of reincarnation. The family you live with today is only a small part of the extended family from your past.

Each person's past link with other people in this life is more like being a member of a far-flung clan, which goes well beyond the close members of today's family. So in this life, other members of your extended family come as schoolmates, friends of childhood, teachers, and the like.

They remain in your dreams because they are a very real part of you. For this lifetime, though, they have chosen a different mission and lifestyle, so you go along your separate paths.

But your inner bond spans time.

The Holy Spirit often works through professional medical people to help us out when we're in trouble.

Freedom from Suffering

I've let my fears really mess me up. Should my goal always be to choose my own way of life no matter what others think of my decisions? Deep down, I know this is true, and yet it's hard to break loose of a feeling that insists I must suffer in this life.

In general, let me say that people will intrude upon our good nature for their own negative purposes if we let them.

It is simply a matter of catching them at their game, then slowly but gradually, over a period of time, letting ourselves be less accessible to them.

It is part of the freedom we can develop for ourselves by adopting a different attitude about What will people think? With practice, we get better at handling the subtle pressures and guilts that are thrown at us, especially if someone is attempting to bend our will to fit their own.

Singing HU either opens us to direct help from Divine Spirit or else gives us the insight on how to handle the next step.

Often, it is enough to sing HU, the ancient name of God, inwardly and silently whenever in the presence of a person who is intruding into our psychic space. Singing HU either opens us to direct help from Divine Spirit or else gives us the insight on how to handle the next step in this situation ourselves.

I want you to know that the love and protection of the ECK, the Holy Spirit, is always with you.

Reasons for Loneliness

I am beset by a terrible loneliness at times but am at a loss to explain it. I am an isolated person—not that I want to be; it just seems to always work out that way. This has been with family, friends, and mates, as well as jobs and people connected to them. Every-

*thing is very short-lived, and it doesn't seem normal.
I do the best I can, but no matter what I do things
are always interrupted and ending all the time.*

*As far back as I can remember, it has always been
this way. Whatever is going on I know has to do with
some past life I lived.*

I greatly appreciated your letter and will try to shed
some light on the feelings of loneliness you spoke of.

Most of the karma we make is from this lifetime,
although periodically there is a long-standing condition hanging on from another lifetime.

Imagine, if you will, the life of a leper in Palestine
shortly before the Christian era. Anyone with a
diagnosis of leprosy faced a life of separation from
his family and friends. The repeated reactions of
horror and disgust by citizens when coming across
lepers would be enough to leave a deep scar for centuries.

Anyone who reincarnates into the present life
from such an existence ought to look on the positive
side. What a blessing to no longer be regarded as a
scourge among people because of a disfiguring disease! Just this thought alone ought to make one
appreciate a healthier body in this lifetime.

Do the Spiritual Exercises of ECK, and I, as the
Inner Master, will work with you.

*Most of the
karma we
make is from
this lifetime,
although
periodically
there is a
long-standing
condition
from another
lifetime.*

SHIFTING YOUR ATTENTION

*A member of my family has always tried to get
me involved with black magic. Lately she has involved herself in a group of psychics who are project-
ing fear and control toward me, my son, and my
daughter. I never made the connection until my
daughter spoke of the voices she kept hearing. What
can I do?*

The only harm that can come to us is that which we allow to happen. To strengthen the spiritual foundation, may I suggest that you and your children either sing HU or do a spiritual exercise together every morning and evening. Also be aware of what kind of rest the children are getting; make sure it is enough right now.

Get into some outside activities that are fun for all of you, if possible. Libraries often have leads on what to do. Whatever you do, put your full attention on the Inner Master, but also get your attention on the brighter things in life. If you fill your consciousness with the positive aspects of Divine Spirit, there is no vacuum where the negative may enter.

A study of dreams can help people learn the spiritual reason their life is as it is, and what they can do to improve their lot.

HEALING THE PAST THROUGH DREAMS

How can one heal oneself in the dream state?

It is possible to get a healing for many conditions, like poor health, emotions, or mental stress. But not always. The study of dreams in Eckankar begins with the fact of past lives. All conditions are due to karma, and some will last a lifetime, such as the loss of a limb. A study of dreams can help people learn the spiritual reason their life is as it is, and what they can do to improve their lot.

A way to heal oneself begins with a spiritual exercise. At bedtime, sing the word HU. Softly sing this ancient name for God for five to ten minutes. Also create a mental picture of your problem. See it as a simple cartoon. Beside it, place another image of the condition as you feel it should be.

The second week, if you've had no luck seeing a past life, do this dream exercise for fifteen or twenty minutes. Take a rest the third week. Repeat this cycle until you succeed.

Keep a record of your dreams. Make a short note about every dream you recall upon awakening. Also be alert during the day for clues about your problem from other people. The Holy Spirit works through them too.

So be aware and listen.

EXPRESS LANE

How soon after the demise of the body can cremation take place? How long does Soul hover near the body before Its journey toward whatever plane is Its destiny?

Cremation may take place anytime after the death of the body. For those on the path of ECK, the Mahanta is immediately on hand to greet the individual on the other side. It is a joyful occasion.

Soul has no reason to wait around for three days, as is the case for those who must get an audience with the Lords of Karma. Someone on the path of ECK goes through the express lane because the Mahanta is with him or her. It is a gift of the Master's love.

WAYS TO HEAL YOURSELF

I used to wake up in a good mood. Now I wake up with negative thoughts. For example, still half-asleep, I will think thoughts like, I'll *get cancer. What is causing this? Are negative entities surrounding me?*

You feel there are entities surrounding you. This is an intrusion, and they are in violation of the spiritual law. I suggest you call or visit a professional counselor and discuss your problem. Ask if he or she can help you rid yourself of them.

This is often the way Divine Spirit works to bring

Keep a record of your dreams. Make a short note about every dream you recall upon awakening.

relief. It can bring a healing through licensed medical practitioners and counselors.

The problem requires you to take a good, close look at yourself. The law is that no one or nothing can harm us unless we let it do so.

Look first at where the attack is coming from, then examine the emotional body to see if a door has not been shut properly. If someone betrays our trust, it is totally our responsibility to slam shut that door against further intrusion. This must be done with more than just the lips, but especially with the heart.

When one betrays our trust and the outcome leaves us a shattered shell, then we have to exert ourselves and fight back with all the ferocity we can muster in the Soul body.

Imagine a heavy door made of the ECK, Divine Spirit. Put all your strength into swinging it shut. Lock it, bolt it, chain it, and then drop a bar across the door. Turn around and walk farther into the Temple of Golden Wisdom. You are walking toward a room of light. Imagine the Mahanta is there to meet you.

Put no more thought upon the dark forces of fear that are now locked out.

> *The problem requires you to take a good, close look at yourself.*

CLAIMS BY OTHERS

I've come across claims by two people who say they are from other planets. What does this mean?

People who just haven't gotten recognition in this lifetime often pretend to be reincarnations of royalty, visitors from space, or some other noble being that puts them above their fellows.

Of course, their past is always of the kind that cannot be checked out by somebody else. Who can go to ancient Egypt and verify that someone was a queen in several centuries B.C.? All that one can do is take these claims upon the authority of the person who makes them, which is a rather doubtful position to be in. Usually these people are harmless and never get more than a ripple of attention from anybody—certainly not from crowds.

One is judged by what he does rather than what he claims to be.

PROTECTION WITH HU

Can you explain briefly what the word HU *means and its use as protection?*

HU, a sacred name for God, is popular among members of Eckankar, especially in Africa. Black magic is a very powerful force there, able to wreak havoc. Someone on the path of ECK who is the object of a curse sings this word *HU* and also pictures a shield of white light between himself and the black magician.

The white light is the Light of God. HU is the Sound of God. The Light and Sound are the two most trusted pillars of protection that one can ever find.

People in Europe, Australia, and the Americas also sing HU quietly or aloud to receive protection from trouble or danger on the street, at work, or in the home.

HU is a powerful defense.

Sing HU quietly or aloud to receive protection from trouble or danger on the street, at work, or in the home.

BECOMING A HAPPIER PERSON

I would like to be happy, but I am often depressed. Can you help?

I received your request for healing, and the matter has been put into the hands of Divine Spirit to do with as It will. As a further suggestion, have you approached professional counseling, besides medical doctors? The Family Service Association is listed in the phone book's white pages in many larger towns.

The reason I offer the suggestion is this: Spirit brings help through a coordination of effort on both the invisible planes and the physical. Spiritually, then, the matter is turned over to Divine Spirit. To complete our willingness to do our own part down here, we make appointments with professional counselors who are trained to dislodge entities.

These are only suggestions. In addition, it will be useful to sing HU softly whenever you feel the negative presence. HU is an ancient name for God and sounds like the word *hue,* but is sung in a long, drawn-out, continuing way.

Spirit brings help through a coordination of effort on both the invisible planes and the physical.

PAST-LIFE READINGS

I've become very interested in past-life regression and am considering getting training in this area. I feel that it would be a valuable service in our medicine fields and would appreciate your guidance in this matter.

You have the freedom to conduct your private life in whatever way you must. But do consider that past-life memory can seriously injure someone if the past is opened without competent guidance. Usually it creates additional deep-seated problems worse than those that led him to seek such help.

The Inner Master gives whatever snatches of the past are important and when the person is emotionally strong enough to take it. That is generally at a very slow, measured pace.

The tangles of past karma are tied in with the

memories of past-life experiences and must be dealt with so carefully. The hypnotist often lacks the spiritual training to deal with karma and pass it off into the Audible Life Stream, the ECK. That's also one reason, in a parallel case, that the suicide rate among psychiatrists is so great.

Many of my friends are very enthused about past-life readings. I am very concerned about this. Is there any benefit to these readings?

Some people need that sort of service until they go beyond that level. Many who are going to readers now will grow into higher understandings of ECK. Then they will not need the rubber crutch provided by past-life readers.

The ECK Masters must make bridges for people from their states of consciousness. For some, the bridge of interest is past-life readings. I started there. People outgrow their childhood, but if that's where they are now, that's where we must meet them.

The path of ECK is not for the God-Realized but for those who wish to reach that station — no matter what their starting point.

The past is past. It holds nothing more for the seeker of God, for he practices the spiritual exercises and lives in the Sound and Light of Divine Spirit.

The inner Master gives what snatches of the past are important when the person is emotionally strong enough.

How HU Can Heal You

I am in desperate need of help. I am totally possessed and controlled by a powerful psychic. This woman feels she owns me — she is actually changing the structure of my brain and my entire personality!

This entity has lodged itself in your consciousness, but there is something which can rid you of it.

I suggest you sing the word *HU* for up to half an hour at a time—but no longer, unless the entity bothers you again. The entity will put up a terrific struggle, but its hold will gradually weaken over a period of several weeks if you sing the word faithfully.

HU, the sacred name for God, opens the channels of healing. This word is empowered to open the door to spiritual healing. Anytime a thought from this entity intrudes upon your mind, sing HU. The entity will repeatedly try to establish itself as a parasite in your consciousness.

HU, the sacred name for God, opens the channels of healing.

It will take diligence to catch its approach and begin the song of HU, which will certainly bring the spiritual travelers of ECK to your aid. The ECK Masters are able to help only if you ask for aid directly!

Also, I suggest you burn any letters from this person and cut off all outer communication. You should have relief after thirty days. Then be prepared to go to a counseling service and ask for help. That is often the way Divine Spirit chooses to help us out of our emotional and mental entanglements.

The real question is: How did she get such a hold on you? One common problem is that we study too many different spiritual paths at the same time and unwittingly open our psychic centers. Alcohol and drugs can have the same effect.

What the ECK Masters Want for You

I am afraid of working with the ECK Masters because a friend of mine says that some people try to control others in the dream state. Can you tell me the truth about this?

I have no interest in controlling other people, since no spiritual purpose is ever served by that.

The negative force can and does come disguised as me as well as other people. To protect yourself against such deception, sing HU or call upon a spiritual leader you know and trust: the Mahanta, Christ, etc.

My mission is to help true seekers find their way home to God. For this reason, all ECK initiates are given wide discretion to run their own inner and outer lives.

All ECK initiates are given wide discretion to run their own inner and outer lives.

Plan for a full, rich life of love and service to God and others.

11
CLIMBING THE
SPIRITUAL LADDER

How do I know my spiritual goal, or purpose, in this lifetime?

You know your *general* purpose is to become a Co-worker with God. So how do you identify your *personal* goal?

Let's say you're a writer planning to write a novel. It is the story of your life. You may drive your story by one of two approaches: by plot or character. Let me explain.

If you plan your life by plot (a master plan), the rest of your life will reflect your spiritual unfoldment at the time of planning. This is a narrow approach. You will reject any experience outside the original plan. It leaves no room for freedom.

A plot-driven story has every detail planned. However, it creates a character (you) whose understanding of life is thin, like a piece of cardboard. Such a person is stiff, afraid of people's opinions. Failure crushes him easily. He or she weighs every act according to an outside authority, such as what people might think.

On the other hand, a character-driven story is like a life guided by the Sound and Light of God. Yes, we do plan. However, in this approach, we recognize the superiority of Soul over any plan. Therefore, if the ECK brings a new direction into our life, which falls outside our original master plan, we contemplate upon it. We are willing to change our direction.

This character-driven approach to living is fresh. It can accept spontaneity. We see the ECK's guidance as a moment-to-moment reality. It is a better guide than our mind, which creates the plot-driven life.

So how do you learn your purpose?

The Mahanta will bring you many right seasons for spiritual growth.

The Mahanta will bring you many right seasons for spiritual growth. Contemplate upon them. Only at the end of your life will you be certain of what your personal goal was and if you have achieved it.

In the meantime, plan for a full, rich life of love and service to God and others.

SPIRITUAL QUEST

Let's say that a person has a dream, goal, or service in mind. How does it fit with his unfoldment to God-Realization?

If an act or plan is selfless, it will aid the individual's spiritual quest.

The ECK, or Holy Spirit, can lift the most common beginning to the highest good. Yet, to succeed, we must first surrender our little self to achieve divine love. How can we do that?

An unselfish dream, goal, or service can help us to the height of spiritual living. To reach it, we must develop a complete love for God. So, we first make an inner agreement to love God, and then life itself will supply what we need to achieve divine love.

Eventually, every dream, goal, or service meets in the Experience of God, which makes us over into a new spiritual being.

ZEST FOR LIFE

I am confused about detachment and how it works in terms of striving for anything, or if we even should strive. Should a person try to get ahead or be successful in worldly terms, or should he just put his efforts into spiritual unfoldment (aside from supporting himself and dependents if he has them)? Is wanting, striving, and desiring just another negative trap?

In the past, too much attention was put on detachment. The wrong definition taken for it was "don't get involved in life." In ECK we are detached, but we are also the great lovers of life. Can it be any other way for a Co-worker with God?

The path of Eckankar is only to enhance our spiritual growth. How does this unfoldment come about? Through daily duties. Yes, it is all right to set goals in business. We can set goals, work to accomplish them, and still be working in the arena of detachment. Detachment means that if our plans don't work out as we think they should, life won't crush us.

The path of ECK ought to bring a zest for life. Each activity contains within it the seed of a spiritual lesson. We do not make spiritual progress by doing as little as possible in life. The individual must make an honest evaluation of his talents, interests, and training to decide what goals he wishes to strive for.

In ECK we are detached, but we are also the great lovers of life.

Every time he sets out to win small goals, he is aware in Soul consciousness that their only purpose is to give him instruction in becoming a citizen of the spiritual hierarchy.

We must first give to life if we expect life to give anything in return. This is the divine law. Life presents a whole series of opportunities. These let us tap into the God Force for aid. This is achieved through the regular practice of the Spiritual Exercises of ECK.

URGE TOWARD GROWTH

I am writing you to get some guidance. As a low-profile type of person, I sometimes have difficulty asserting myself. Sometimes getting ahead seems to mean stepping on others, and I don't want to do this. But I wonder: What's the balance between being active and waiting for what I want to be provided by the ECK?

Many others have the same problem as you in resolving how to live the spiritual life and not get caught up in power plays over those less able than us.

Soul is a joyful, creative, and active being.

We are not passive people, content to let others do to us what they will. Soul is a joyful, creative, and active being.

Note the word *creative*. It means that we decide what we want to achieve in our lives, and then we make step-by-step goals to accomplish our ends.

Whatever profession you are in, you will feel an urge toward growth. This is natural for Soul. We do all we can to keep the goodwill of others as we go about gathering our rich spiritual experiences in this life. But we do recognize limits.

Some people take advantage of us. They make us puppets and allow for no growth in our development. In such an event, make careful plans to achieve your goals where you work (further study toward accreditation), or investigate a new place of employment.

You are unhappy where you are. That means you are ready to change your outlook to something broader on how to live a more spiritual life.

Earn Self-Mastery

I've been puzzled for years over the difference between success in the spiritual life and that of the physical life. Although I'm an ECK initiate, my personal life in terms of employment and finances is literally in shambles. You would think that spiritual advances would give some light on my life's work.

Others have seen themselves in what has happened to you. I have several letters on my desk that ask, "We've got the Sound and Light of God; now what?" Then go out and earn self-mastery, I would say. But then comes the natural question: How? And so the mind goes.

In the meantime there are the regular problems that used to confront us. If someone caught us in a moment of honesty and asked, "How is your life different from what it was before you stepped on the path of Eckankar?" what could we say? Surely, there must be a way to put into words and practice the benefits of ECK!

Step one: Let's look around and see what surrounds our state of consciousness. Meaning: What are we doing with our time every day, and what are we learning from it, if anything? What do we expect from living? What do we expect after we finish living in

You are unhappy where you are. That means you are ready to change your outlook to something broader on how to live a more spiritual life.

this body? If the answer to that comes into focus, then we could say, I know my spiritual mission in life.

Tonight I played Ping-Pong with someone who is better than I am. This is good, for there is always someone better than we are in something. Fortunately he also lives close by and enjoys the game for exercise. There is a need for exercise for the body just as there is a need for the spiritual exercise for Soul.

It's the little things in life, my friend. Our mission is to find our place in the spiritual community and serve God as a carrier of the Light and Sound.

Thinking from the End

What does "thinking from the end" mean?

The ancient Greeks were experts in this technique. It means the ability to visualize your desires and give them life by filling them with feeling. Think of a goal, then set intermediate steps leading to it.

To reach the state of God-Realization, put yourself in the ECK Master's shoes.

To reach the state of God-Realization, put yourself in the ECK Master's shoes. Each time you confront a problem, ask: "What would the Mahanta do in this situation?" Then do it. That's thinking from the end.

The ECK, Divine Spirit, is continually pressing forward for expression through you. Thinking from the end is the creative process that makes life a controllable and enjoyable thing.

How Can You Be a Lover of Life?

How can I live my life less in the grips of power and more in the grace of love?

It is easy to see that those with compassion have learned to love by the trials of suffering, now and in some time past. Coleridge said, "He prayeth best who loveth best / All things both great and small."

A quiet life is all most of us hope for, but the ECK takes a little of us at first, then a little more, until Divine Spirit has all of us.

Two kinds of people are on the path of ECK: those who love the Mahanta above all, and those who love themselves more. The Outer Master is the main channel of the ECK to bring about reactions in initiates, but the spiritual tests only unmask the individual for what he is: a lover of God or a servant of power.

With love, I am always with you.

FINDING YOUR CYCLE

Please tell me about cycles of activity and rest. When I feel reluctant to get involved in outer activities in Eckankar, I am not sure what this means.

There are rest points in eternity, and one often finds a cycle of outer activity followed by seeking out quietness. It's a natural part of life, and one must not be too concerned about it.

Those on the path of ECK work in their communities as individuals serving the ECK. One can always be a listening ear as well, as a silent vehicle for Divine Spirit, when the occasion comes. We can serve as vehicles for Spirit by just being ourselves.

There are rest points in eternity, and one often finds a cycle of outer activity followed by seeking out quietness.

SPIRITUAL SUCCESS

I have been disappointed in my experiences so far in ECK. I also have felt a great imbalance in my life. Isn't ECK supposed to straighten this out?

The approach to success in spiritual things is like success in high-school sports. Some youths trying out for basketball dribble the ball down the street. They touch, bounce, and toss the basketball until it becomes an extension of themselves.

The same is true of football players. In fact, some coaches make errant players carry the ball around campus the week following an error that lost the game for the team.

It also takes a complete commitment in learning Soul Travel or meeting the Mahanta, the Inner Master. This is something nobody can give to you. The motivation must be from within yourself. After you develop the self-discipline to do the Spiritual Exercises of ECK faithfully, then you can look for results.

After you develop the self-discipline to do the Spiritual Exercises of ECK faithfully, then you can look for results.

The same discipline is needed if one wants to become a doctor. A few weeks of halfhearted study does not create an M.D. Years of self-sacrifice are usually the price of success. What does the medical student hope to accomplish that drives him toward his goal? For some it is merely money, but for others it is to make life easier for others living on this planet. But whatever is behind his drive, he has drive.

Your approach to the spiritual exercises can be more flexible and experimental. The guidepost is a monthly report—to yourself, if necessary. Keep a log that lists insights or dreams, or something that happened in contemplation. If your log shows no success within a month, try a new spiritual exercise.

There's a definite spiritual current in Eckankar. It's like climbing a mountain. Take your time so you can acclimate to the altitude.

CONSCIOUS EVOLUTION

Recently I have become interested in subliminal tapes. Is there any spiritual harm to using them? How do they fit in with spiritual goals?

The problem with subliminal tapes is that they bypass the conscious mind. You're letting somebody tinker with your mind without any idea of what is being planted in it without your knowledge.

The people who sell these tapes may have high ethics, but we get into the bad habit of trusting people whose major interest is in selling tapes, rather than in our welfare. Our defenses are let down. The first time some trickster puts a hypnotic suggestion on the tape (e.g., buy another tape), we are trapped.

Subliminal tapes run us toward mechanical evolution. Soul's desire is conscious evolution.

Some of my friends go to a medium. This brought to mind all the spiritual and not-so-spiritual programs available these days. How do they differ from Eckankar and Soul Travel?

Mediums attract a lot of curiosity seekers, but it's nothing more than spiritual window-shopping. They're making the rounds. If the hoopla changes as often as the monthly TV programming, the medium holds the crowd. Otherwise, the crowd leaves for new hoopla.

This sort of thing is needed for those people who must have the experience of finding a short-haul guru.

Too many think in terms of "Give me God-Realization, and true fulfillment will be mine." But hardly a one has thought about what he will do after that great moment comes. One finds that with spiritual liberation comes total freedom and total responsibility.

Who will go to the store on Thursday for the groceries? Will the fix-it man accept divine love in trade for repairing the car's muffler? Somehow,

One finds that with spiritual liberation comes total freedom and total responsibility.

there's a big gap in people's minds about what they are today and what they'll be once they experience the most sacred of occasions in the presence of the Sugmad, as God is called in the ancient teachings.

I don't want to disillusion anybody about the experience of God, but they ought to be somewhat realistic about it when it does come.

Is there any problem attending meetings of more than one spiritual group at the same time? What does this do to one's spiritual development?

First of all, don't ever let any other person tell you how to run your universe, including me. You were sincere in wanting to know my advice to ECK initiates in regard to getting involved with other groups, so I offer it for your consideration.

You alone must make the decision of whether or not to be a member of more than one group at a time. I do however ask that the teachings from other groups be left outside the ECK classes, because two different teachings do not mix. Each discipline emanates from a unique vibrational current, even as each individual has a personal aura.

A person who throws himself wholeheartedly in two directions and still hopes to do either of them justice is simply fooling himself.

A person who throws himself wholeheartedly in two directions and still hopes to do either of them justice is simply fooling himself. Problems come up that seem to be from no rightful origin. They arise from the conflict of two distinct paths that each have their own force field. When the two come into proximity of each other, there is a clash in the invisible worlds that works out in the physical world as problems that seem to have no reason for being.

None of these problems are of such a nature that

you cannot deal with them if you are a strong person inside. Each individual's circumstances are different.

The general principle is that two paths do not mix if one tries to live both of them to the hilt at the same time. But you can try to blend the two, and see what there is for learning. I would rather have people do something and get experience than be sitting on their hands while life passes them by.

SPIRITUAL GOALS AND RELIGIONS

What's the purpose of religions? How do they help Soul reach Its spiritual goals?

Religions have been developed to aid mankind in reaching God. Each religion was and is a channel of ECK, the Holy Spirit, to spiritually uplift a certain band of consciousness. However, too often religions get away from their original purpose and begin to manipulate society.

When truth comes into a person or a religion, it makes a passive state active.

When truth comes into a person or a religion, it makes a passive state active. In this active state, people are driven toward action. Here's the rub: They act from their own imperfect states of consciousness.

One of the most destructive forces unleashed by the pure water of truth is some people's lust for power. They wish to control others. So truth in expression becomes a highly charged accelerator that fires up the engines of karma. As people work off their karma, truth expresses itself through their hard-won spiritual lessons.

To expand that last thought: When truth enters the vessel of a person or a religion, things begin to pop. As far as we're concerned, truth does not operate in a vacuum. Therefore, people who've been touched a little by truth try to express it in their daily lives:

within a family structure, a business, or a religion.

A religion is composed of layers and layers of people with different states of consciousness. Some of those individuals act nobly toward others, while a few try to use truth for personal gain. The latter like power politics and cause a lot of problems for others before their karmic engines run out of steam.

Eckankar has the same faults within its infrastructure. That's because it too is composed of many different kinds of people. Some are always trying to limit the truth that comes through Eckankar. The rest of us do all we can to reopen the channel of truth. A never-ending struggle, but worth the trouble for many people like you.

OUR UNFOLDMENT AS SOUL

In the high spiritual worlds, above the realm of time and space, how does Soul progress?

It doesn't in the way we think of movement. The most we can say is that Soul unfolds spiritually.

As you suggest, in a world where space or time does not exist, there can be no travel or progress. Travel or progress means going from one point in space to a second point, and that also requires duration.

Space, time, and matter collapse when Soul reaches the Soul Plane, the first of the high spiritual worlds. Spiritual development continues, however.

Space, time, and matter collapse when Soul reaches the Soul Plane, the first of the high spiritual worlds. Spiritual development continues, however.

The problem is human language. It originated on the Mental Plane, the last refuge of space and time. Since our spoken communication is based on the concepts of space and time, which are limited, we must use limited terms to address even those things that are beyond limitations.

For this reason the spoken word, even in ECK, is useful only to a certain point in learning truth. Finally, we must learn by direct perception.

EVOLUTION

Can you explain evolution?

Evolution is a guess by science about how a life-form changed since its beginning. A key word is *change.*

Evolution is the idea that everything changes over time. One example is the family of elephants, which includes the mammoth of thousands of years ago. The mammoth and the elephant came from the same ancestor. Today the mammoth is gone, and the elephant remains.

Change is natural. So evolution fits right in with the ECK teachings.

TOWARD GOD

How can I reach God-Realization if I don't know what it is or what to aim at?

A definition of God-Realization in all its details would fill volumes. But, in short, it is the state of seeing, knowing, and being from the highest spiritual plane.

That is one definition. Getting to that state is a whole other matter, of course. Here are a few guidelines on how to reach God-Realization: (1) do everything in the name of the Mahanta or the ECK, (2) do even the smallest act with love and attention to detail, and (3) above all, give others the right to find their own way to God.

A definition of God-Realization in all its details would fill volumes. But, in short, it is the state of seeing, knowing, and being from the highest spiritual plane.

How do you accomplish that? The road to God begins with the Spiritual Exercises of ECK. Do them with love. Also pay close attention to the daily instructions, insights, and details that the Mahanta will give you about reaching God Consciousness. Most of the training comes via the inner channels. Yet the details must prove themselves in everyday life.

PERSONAL GOALS

How do you tell when a goal you're striving for is the right one, and the methods you are using are also right?

One must have trust in the ECK, and then follow through to manifest the good things in life.

One must have trust in the ECK, and then follow through to manifest the good things in life. When you simply act "as if" you'd get your goal and trying for it hurts no one else in any way, that is one test of whether something you do is right or not.

I think you used good sense and used the principles to allow Divine Spirit to manifest for you what It would. Nothing wrong in that. Keep on with your personal spiritual experiments in ECK.

FINE-TUNING

After years of experience with the Light and Sound of God, I guess I have gotten used to being in Its presence, and It's not as vividly obvious as It used to be. What is happening?

You're getting into an area where there's fine-tuning to be done on the inner. This is why people have experiences when they first get on the path of Eckankar and later they go away. They've become used to their own state of being at that level.

I illustrated a similar principle in my book *The Wind of Change* with the story on invisibility. You can, for your experience sometime, come into such harmony with the outer vibrations of the people around you that you walk among them in such a way that you don't disturb their field force. Their senses aren't alerted, so for all purposes you are invisible to them. What you've really done is raise your vibration.

Before you come to this understanding in your spiritual unfoldment, you get used to your dream state and your spiritual experiences so they no longer register upon the mind. The mind is the vehicle usually used to translate the vision of the higher worlds down to the lower worlds, but if the mind gets too numb or tired or accustomed to the experiences, it simply doesn't register them anymore.

So we have to be creative in our spiritual exercises. We approach everything in a fresh, new way, like a child would. I do this sometimes too because I want to do certain research or put myself in a discipline so I can easily slip back into a state of remembering the other planes. Usually I don't bother, but sometimes when I'm writing I have to verify things or get ideas.

We approach everything in a fresh, new way, like a child would.

But most important is to live here, in the present.

Open Your Eyes

I am an eighty-seven-year-old who has not yet succeeded in opening my Third Eye. What do you recommend?

You asked to have the Tisra Til, the Spiritual Eye, opened. When it begins to open, you start to have experience with the Light of ECK in some manner or other, or else with the Sound. When both come together in a single matrix within the Spiritual Eye, the fortunate one is seeing the Mahanta, the Inner Master, who has stationed himself there to purify the negative stream that wants always to flow into the student.

Are you aware of any Light or Sound during contemplation or the dream state?

The question then is: Are you aware of any Light or Sound during contemplation or the dream state? The Light may be a blue star, disc, or globe; It may even be white, yellow, or green. The Sound may resemble a rushing wind, a symphony, a humming of bees, or the sound of a flute. Some hear the distant chirping of crickets. Others may have none of these manifestations but simply recall a meeting with one of the ECK Masters.

Other people find something quite different when the Spiritual Eye is opened. An awareness grows, not of the other worlds, but of the love and protection of the Mahanta. It settles about their shoulders like a warm cloak of love. Others carry a knowingness that their spiritual lives are directed by the great hand of the ECK, the Holy Spirit.

So, you see, when the Third Eye opens there can be a wide variety of ways that Soul becomes aware of it.

HELP WITH TAKEOFF

It has been ten years since I began studying Eckankar. I have not to my knowledge had any spiritual experiences, such as seeing the Light of God. I love the ECK teachings, but I'm frustrated that I'm not able to have these experiences.

Paul Twitchell, the modern-day founder of Eckankar, mentioned in his writings the feeling of anticipation one has when going to meet a loved one at the airport. I have had that feeling for a long time but cannot take many more canceled flights.

I know I have to be patient and persistent, but I'm very tired. I have an awful lot to learn, so please, will you help me get started?

It was good to hear from you. In response to the lack of success in Eckankar with the spiritual exercises, I can only say that each person is unique, and Divine Spirit brings him along at the proper speed for him.

Success comes from one's exercise of self-discipline. Contemplation must be done with joyful expectation. Before dropping off to sleep at night, it's possible to make a request of the Inner Master like this: "I give you permission to take me to that Temple of Golden Wisdom that fits my spiritual state, or any place else you choose." Then go to sleep and forget the permission you gave to the Mahanta.

It is a spiritual discipline to do the spiritual exercises daily.

Success comes from one's exercise of self-discipline.

Go at Your Own Pace

I am not a student of Eckankar but my husband is. I have come to realize that he is in a changed state of consciousness. I've read in some of the ECK books that one person can drag the other down, and I don't want to be that sort of person, since it would put a strain on our marriage. How do I go about letting him grow at his own rate and me at mine?

Thank you for your letter of concern. When one's love for God is so strong and leads us into unfamiliar areas, it is best to go slowly and give love and good-will to all life.

ECK moves to bring harmony to families. By *ECK* I mean the Holy Spirit as you are more familiar with it. Stay with the Catholic teachings of your youth. The love and protection of Divine Spirit surmount any distinctions of religious paths if the seeker is sincere in wanting the experience of God.

The love and protection of Divine Spirit surmount any distinctions of religious paths if the seeker is sincere in wanting the experience of God.

Don't be alarmed, for you are unfolding along with your husband, even though you are more comfortable in your childhood religion. After all, any religious teaching must fit you; not you, it. If you'll accept the fact that you can see the spiritual unfoldment of your spouse because his is only a reflection of your own, you will enjoy your family in your daily duties as well as recreation.

The first two years of membership in Eckankar are purposely set aside for one to study its suitability to oneself. After two years of study one can better make the decision of whether or not to follow Eckankar or Catholicism. The choice must be based on what you learn is right for you.

ATTITUDE OF THE LOVING HEART

After I got my Second Initiation in Eckankar, I immediately had a bad car accident. Is this part of the initiation? I am concerned about getting any more of them.

Please do not feel that great troubles are a natural aftermath of receiving an ECK initiation.

When one gets the initiation on any level, the ECK, the Audible Life Stream, flows through him in a greater amount. The Holy Spirit uplifts and purifies the consciousness of the individual so that it fits the new level of spiritual understanding that he has reached.

One can have a smooth route through most initiations by listening to the subtle promptings of Divine Spirit trying to steer him past unnecessary karma. The attitude that one can develop is of loving awareness of how the ECK principles are now working in a greater degree in his life.

It is our attitudes that have caused karma. Thus you can see that as quickly as we can identify and let go of those attitudes that harm us, we will move smoothly into the spiritual worlds.

At each level of unfoldment, we realize that we've outgrown some of our previous attitudes. They have no part in the new spiritual consciousness that we have earned. They must go, or we must meet the situation until the lesson is absorbed.

I certainly would not walk around with a black shadow over my head. Instead one can look to the Light and Sound of ECK with a loving heart and simpleness in spirit, like a young child trusting its parent to bring it all it needs to survive in life.

An attitude of the loving heart can dissolve much of the unnecessary karma. It becomes powerless to touch us because of the protection of the Mahanta.

How Is an Eckankar Initiation Different?

How are the ECK initiations different from those of other paths?

A man told me of an acquaintance of his, who was sixty-seven. He had traveled to Tibet, China, South America, and all ends of the earth to study under the great unknown healers among us. In the process of his education, he took numerous initiations of power and light, some of which would astound the orthodox mind.

An attitude of the loving heart can dissolve much of the unnecessary karma. It becomes powerless to touch us because of the protection of the Mahanta.

Yet all these minor initiations, which are prerequisites to the ECK initiations, had left him an emotional, social, and financial cripple. None of those ceremonies had the power to integrate the different parts of his being and blend them into something that would bridge for him the void between the visible and invisible planes.

Thus he was the receiver of psychic powers, but spiritually he could not put one foot ahead of the other and walk without tripping.

The Eckankar initiation is a quiet thing.

The Eckankar initiation is a quiet thing. It sets into motion the erratic energy from past-life karma, the impetus that lets one come within a centimeter of the goal only to lose it by an unconscious self-destructive nature.

Those who know little about the initiations think of them as so much foolish hogwash. They don't know that one earns them dearly. That's why they're so important in one's spiritual unfoldment.

THE USE OF VISUALIZATION

What benefits can visualization bring in spiritual growth?

Everyone's experiences are different. You may have a hard time getting to a certain level spiritually. Once you get there, you're so happy to be there that you don't want to leave. You get caught up in a kind of spiritual lethargy. Something which will help you pull yourself along are the spiritual exercises, which are, after all, visualization techniques.

In the ECK book *Talons of Time,* author Paul Twitchell talks about the Time Makers and their role here in the lower worlds. You may have a spiritual plan for yourself with a starting point, an interval where you try to carry it out, and an ending point where you reach your goal. The Time Makers, or the negative power, try to capture Soul somewhere in the middle and immobilize It. It can show up in a number of different ways: procrastination, lethargy. It serves simply to stop Soul from unfolding.

You can use the visualization techniques to pull yourself free from the mud.

MAKING THE CLIMB EASIER

Can you give me some help on how to make it easier to move to the next initiation?

Each new level of ECK initiation is entering into the vortex of a greater vibration from the ECK. To make it easier upon ourselves, the old rule is to "give up and let go." That means putting aside all our preconceived notions of what is or is not in line with the initiation.

The ECK, the Holy Spirit, always does that which is right for the moment. Each person is treated as an individual. Our opinion of the value of the ECK's workings is of no concern to It, for the thing that must be done will be done regardless.

It is seen that there is only a hairbreadth difference between the material and spiritual planes. Some cannot tell the difference between them, because it is not the two planes that are so different at all, but our state of consciousness in regard to them. All is therefore of Divine Spirit. The degree to which we realize that is the degree to which we aspire for even higher things.

The Mahanta is concerned only that the individual shall unfold in some way. The goal is ECK Mastership, but on the road one must first master

You can use the visualization techniques to pull yourself free from the mud.

Being a Master implies having earned the power to control our destiny.

the Physical Plane, then the Astral, and so on.

What does it mean to be a Master? It means to be in full control of the conditions on any plane on which we have earned the recognition as a Master. Being a Master implies having earned the power to control our destiny.

A direct and simple way to God is to find someone or something to love every day.

12
SOUL TRAVEL AND THE SPIRITUAL MASTERS

What's the purpose of Soul Travel? Is it more important than learning divine love, for example?

I am really more interested in having an individual open up to divine love than to achieve anything else, including Soul Travel. Soul Travel is the natural way for expansion of consciousness and travel into the spiritual worlds of God. Yet all that it is, is one means available for you to find the love of God.

The path of ECK is much broader than Soul Travel, of course. There are many ways that Divine Spirit, the ECK, expresses Itself to the human race, but many of the ways seem so commonplace that the average person doesn't see or hear them anymore.

This includes all the sounds of nature: the sound of a gentle breeze, rustling leaves in autumn, the chirping of crickets, the purring of a cat, the low hum of a refrigerator, the laughing of children at play, and hundreds of other examples.

You mentioned your practice of former times

Soul Travel is the natural way for expansion of consciousness and travel into the spiritual worlds of God.

where you went off by yourself to commune with God and nature. If you could ever recapture that, you would find much of the spiritual unfoldment you are looking for.

Our society admires more mental things today: food for thought—either in writings or speeches. From this material, the Living ECK Master looks for an avenue to Soul that will result in the human mind stepping aside for a moment, letting the miracle of divine illumination occur.

You do not have to Soul Travel to be successful in ECK. Another way to God-Realization is to give tender love and care to every action, because of your love for God.

A direct and simple way to God is to find someone or something to love every day.

A direct and simple way to God is to find someone or something to love every day. Then, at bedtime, let your thoughts gently drift back to this moment of love in your day. Contemplate on that with love and joy. Your contemplative exercises can be as simple as that.

How Do You Use Your Imagination?

I've heard that we should use our imagination to Soul Travel, but can we use too much imagination? Sometimes I'll have an experience and am not sure whether I've made it up.

To imagine Soul Travel is the first thing one must do before actually getting out of the body.

A girl who plays second base for a baseball team in town is called a "natural." But she works hard at her fielding and hitting. Her brothers are all good ball players, and in her mind she imagines herself every bit as good as they are. And so she *is* good, not only because of her imagination, but mainly because she practices harder than the other girls on the team.

Keep on imagining that you do Soul Travel, and one day you will suddenly do it. You will have no more doubt about the difference between imagination and Soul Travel. Wait and see!

USES OF SOUL TRAVEL

How and for what purpose were the pyramids constructed?

Your question about the pyramids is a real chance for you to learn Soul Travel.

Soul learns by doing things. Studies show that a person learns faster by doing, rather than by just listening to others. If your question about the pyramids is more than idle curiosity, I'll get you started in your research.

Soul learns by doing things.

The historical starting point for the pyramids goes back to Atlantis, the continent that once included the Bahamas, where you now live. It was an advanced civilization that boasted giant pyramids. They were the inspiration for later replicas in Egypt and Central America.

The Atlanteans had developed science beyond anything known today, including exotic means of space travel for the colonization of nearby planets. The huge continent eventually broke up and sank, but only after many years of cataclysms that left little trace of its former greatness.

During the final series of earthquakes and volcanoes about 12,000 B.C., the Atlanteans packed their goods and fled to Europe, Africa, and the Americas. They took along the culture of their motherland, thus accounting for the similarity of architecture and customs found in widely scattered places like Egypt and

Central America, both of which are sites of colossal pyramids.

The Egyptian pyramids and the smaller monuments built in the same complex were mainly for religious reasons. After the death of the pharaoh, the Egyptians took it for granted that the king would continue with the duties and rituals he had enjoyed as ruler in his earthly life. Therefore, the pyramids held a duplicate of all possessions he had owned on earth, for use in the afterlife.

Viewed from above, the shape of a pyramid suggests a flood of light from heaven shining upon the earth. But if one looks at it from the ground level, the pyramid seems more like a stairway to heaven.

The grandest pyramids were from the golden age of the Old Kingdom of Egypt. The builders still had knowledge of highly advanced Atlantean measuring and cutting methods. This somewhat explains the remarkably close fit of stones in the Great Pyramid. But if we even mentioned antigravity devices as building tools, critics would use that as a blade against ECK doctrines, which care only about showing Soul the way out of this material prison.

Seekers go to the inner planes for their own understanding of ancient world history as it really happened.

Today's archaeologists say that the pyramids were built by slaves, who dragged tons of stone up temporary ramps along the sides of the pyramids. This is certainly true of the later pyramids, which were of a cruder construction than those of the Old Kingdom of about 2500 B.C.

In his talks, the Living ECK Master usually avoids talking about the scientific marvels of Atlantis. He would rather have spiritual seekers go to the inner planes for their own understanding of ancient world history as it really happened.

Here's the way to do that: First, learn all you can

about the pyramids from books on Egypt and Atlantis. A strong desire to learn ancient history will tell the Mahanta that you really do want to know about them. Second, take any questions that come up in your research to the Mahanta in contemplation.

To get you started, look for these books in a good library: *Atlantis: The Antediluvian World* by I. Donnelly (New York: Harper, 1949), *The Testimony of the Spade* by Geoffrey Bibby (New York: A. Knopf, 1956), and *The History of Atlantis* by Lewis Spence (Philadelphia: David McKay & Company, 1927).

The reference librarian may be able to help you if the books are not in the library's listings. Or you may visit a book dealer who specializes in finding out-of-print books, since these are old titles.

Saturate yourself with the subject of the pyramids. Take questions to the Mahanta, the Inner Master. Chant a sacred word, such as the name for God, HU, and ask for answers to come in the best way. They may come during Soul Travel or in a dream. Or the Mahanta may guide you to a new book.

Research into the past for a study of the pyramids is a wonderful idea because underneath the wealth of history is a pattern of the ancient people who either obeyed or abused the laws of Divine Spirit. Their mistakes can benefit you, if you learn to avoid them.

I hope this gets you going in the right direction. Whether or not you do such in-depth research is entirely up to you. Frankly, if it's done leisurely, a study of this sort can be highly enjoyable.

Chant a sacred word, such as the name for God, HU, and ask for answers to come in the best way.

DO ANIMALS SOUL TRAVEL?

I would like to know if animals such as lions, cows, and dogs have Soul Travel experiences.

Some animals do. They're the same as people, in that animals have many different levels of consciousness.

*Like us,
all animals
dream. Some
remember,
many don't.
Specially
gifted
ones, like
spiritually
advanced
people, do
Soul Travel.*

Like us, all animals dream. Some remember, many don't. Specially gifted ones, like spiritually advanced people, do Soul Travel. In time, scientific research will be able to expand its knowledge of what happens when people and animals sleep.

You can begin exploring your interests in these fields of knowledge through dreams or Soul Travel. Eventually, science will catch up to the knowledge of those who already can explore the spiritual states of living beings—human or animal—by Soul Travel.

WHEN YOU DON'T REMEMBER

Why am I unconscious of any spiritual or Soul Travel experiences I may be having during contemplation or at other times?

First, I would like to ask, Do you have any recall of either the Light or Sound of ECK?

Have you had any dream with the Mahanta, the Inner Master, at any time? Some people don't until several years after they begin the study of Eckankar. Others would frankly be more comfortable in another study, for there is one provided by God to fit each of us.

What would happen to your emotions if you were to recall a Soul Travel experience before proper preparations were made to build spiritual stamina? It is hard to say.

For instance, a woman today wanted to see a past life where she had been an initiate of the Living ECK Master of the times. She carried a haunting fear that she had done something terrible to him in that life-time and that the consequences had come with her into the present time. After months without an answer, the past records opened to show her as an initiate of the Tibetan ECK Master Rebazar Tarzs.

She had gained a high degree of unfoldment then, but one willful act against him—without cause—had thrown her off the path of Light and Sound. She saw the exact violation, which I won't dwell on here. The point of this example is that the truth almost drove her to despair.

Several weeks ago, an impatient member of Eckankar begged to have his karma speeded up. He wanted to advance rapidly on the path to make up time lost in recent years by squandering pearls of opportunity. He has no idea what is he asking. The path of ECK is only for the Soul that is sincere about returning to God. My only function is to give It assistance in Its own efforts toward that supreme goal.

The path of ECK is only for the Soul that is sincere about returning to God.

I won't hold you to the way of ECK if you feel it is not for you. You are not ready for Soul Travel now. It would not be good for you. In *ECKANKAR: Illuminated Way Letters* Paul Twitchell stated: "There are those who cannot see anything in ECK beyond what is known as Soul Travel alone. They limit themselves to the possibility of falling into the psychic trap of Kal Niranjan, the king of the negative power." Look to your dreams for one month, keep a dream notebook, and see what results you get.

How can I better remember my inner experiences?

Do not be too concerned if your memory of the inner experiences goes more into the background for a while. The ECK Masters work with the individual through the different planes in order to maintain balance in the physical, everyday life.

Look to the Mahanta for spiritual insight. This may come through gentle nudgings on how to try something new with the spiritual exercises. Do those things in your contemplations that you like to do.

It is often very effective to finish contemplation as usual, then, when going to bed for the night, simply say to the Mahanta in everyday language: "I give you permission to take me where I am ready to go. This is in your hands." Go to sleep without another thought of it.

Take your time, and don't hurry. It is better to go slowly and learn the lessons of Divine Spirit well.

Take your time, and don't hurry. It is better to go slowly and learn the lessons of Divine Spirit well.

HUMAN REACTIONS

When I Soul Travel, I sometimes wake up feeling physically ill. Why?

This is the reaction of the human consciousness to the infusion of Divine Spirit. It is similar to the reaction that occurs when a wire is stretched across the positive and negative poles of a battery. Spirit will have Its way, and after several months this discomfort will pass.

BEYOND SOUL TRAVEL

Although I had many Soul Travel experiences when I was young, I am no longer able to Soul Travel or see the inner light. What is the cause of this? I do not understand my spiritual blindness.

It is a great privilege for Soul to incarnate into the physical plane. The lessons of Soul that are gained here cannot be done as well elsewhere.

You have contact with the Sound and Light of ECK. This brings with it an assurance and confidence that allows one to live each moment with fullness of heart.

Just about everyone benefits from the expansion of consciousness, also known as Soul Travel. This may come as an increased awareness and insight into everyday situations, or spiritual understanding. Not always will one experience sensational out-of-body travels.

This is better, because when one reaches the Soul Plane, there is no more Soul Travel.

Soul Travel brings Soul through the lower worlds—the Astral, Causal, Mental, and Etheric Planes—until one reaches the Soul Plane. There Soul Travel stops because it is limited to the regions of matter, energy, space, and time. Here, one begins to work with seeing, knowing, and being. It is a whole new ball game.

The veil lifts gradually from our spiritual eyesight as we become ready to look farther into the spiritual realities. The pace is measured so that the individual can maintain his balance while still living in the physical body.

Soul Travel brings Soul through the lower worlds— the Astral, Causal, Mental, and Etheric Planes— until one reaches the Soul Plane. Here, one begins to work with seeing, knowing, and being.

Soul and the Bodies

I recently read about the phenomenon of a physical body changing hands between two Souls, with the new Soul being called a walk-in. *Can you tell me more?*

There are walk-ins for several different reasons, but you can read more about this in books at the library or on the newsstands.

When someone puts too much attention on a
negative thing such as walk-ins, he himself could
become party to such an intrusion either as victim
or perpetrator. This is why I put no emphasis on it
in the outer works of ECK.

*Can Soul operate more than one physical body at
a time on this planet?*

Yes, It can. But it is a skill usually reserved for
those who have put a great deal of energy into spiritual unfoldment, like the ECK Masters.

Some of the old saints could run two or more
bodies at once. A case in point is Padre Pio, who gave
his whole life in service to God. How many are willing
and able to do that?

Can Soul Get Lost?

*For many years now I've had a certain fear of Soul
Travel. I've heard about some spiritual seekers being
in awesome battles in the other worlds. Not having
enormous faith in my own fighting abilities, I wonder
what would happen if I lost the battle and were killed
or captured. Do accidents occur while traveling the
Far Country, like being separated from the Mahanta
and getting lost forever?*

First, not everyone fights in such inner battles.
Among the more adventurous dream travelers are
those born in January. They may often fight such
battles. But other people, even some born in January,
choose inner experiences that better suit their peace-
ful natures. You are one of these.

No Soul is forever separated from the Mahanta
through some accidental mix-up of signals on the

*No Soul is
forever
separated
from the
Mahanta
through some
accidental
mix-up of
signals on
the inner
planes.*

inner planes. The "Far Country" may not be the best description of the nearness of your own inner worlds. You cannot become lost in them, because the Far Country is your personal universe.

The Mahanta is simply there to acquaint you with your own worlds of being.

Can You Overcome Fear of Soul Travel?

When fear stops you from continuing a Soul Travel experience, can you overcome that fear?

First of all, I'm glad to see you using the word *continuing.* It means that you have at least had a little experience with Soul Travel.

You are right, it is only fear that stops us from progress with Soul Travel. What happens when you love someone or something with your whole heart? Right, fear is pushed out of your mind!

Therefore, can you go into contemplation by putting a thought into your heart about something you did once that made you happier than you'd ever been before? Then take with you the thought: I love God with all that is within me.

I hope that this will help you get over your fear. It is quite a natural thing, but you will see it growing less powerful as you keep on with the spiritual exercises.

Belief in Your Experiences

How can you tell the difference between an out-of-body experience and a very vivid dream?

When it happens, you'll know. You won't need to

The Mahanta is simply there to acquaint you with your own worlds of being.

ask anyone to verify a Soul Travel experience, because it is literally out of this world.

A word of caution, however. Should you have one, be most careful with whom you share it. You are the genuine authority on that experience. Unless the person you confide in has Soul traveled, he or she may dismiss your experience as only a vivid dream.

Don't let anyone make you doubt your spiritual experiences.

Don't let anyone make you doubt your spiritual experiences.

WHEN YOU PASS ON

I would like to learn to Soul Travel in order to be prepared when I die. I am a little afraid of it now and would like it to be a joyful experience, since I am quite old and may be passing soon.

The ECK works in Its own way with each of us. It will bring whatever is right for our spiritual progress.

Some initiates never have Soul traveled nor seen a particular manifestation of Divine Spirit, such as the Blue Light. We are all different.

It is of singular importance for us to contact the Mahanta, the Inner Master. Depending upon our station in life, we may become aware of either Light, Sound, or the appearance of the Inner Master. These are inward expressions.

Other valid signs of the ECK reported by initiates include a knowingness of divine intervention during the waking life. Otherwise it can be an impression of help from a mysterious source that one immediately accepts as the Holy Spirit.

It is not good if someone has too many striking inner experiences, because all they may do is put him out of step with his friends and family. The secret of

ECK is to live in step with all of life if that is possible.

The moment of passing from this life, or what is called translation, can be a wonderful experience, the highlight of Soul's chapter on earth. There is nothing special that one on the path of ECK has to do to prepare outwardly for the event. Make the usual arrangements for the disposal of the physical remains. Leave it in the hands of Divine Spirit to decide when the body is no longer suitable as a house for Soul.

I will be with you at the moment chosen for this occasion. This is usually a pleasant and spiritually invigorating event in one's life. As one enters into it, there come the memories of having done it before. All fear and doubt vanish. The radiant form of the Mahanta appears and takes the individual to the worlds of light and love.

The radiant form of the Mahanta appears and takes the individual to the worlds of light and love.

DESIRE TO SOUL TRAVEL

What can I do to get colorful, vivid, exciting, and dramatic inner experiences like the ones I've heard about?

Those inner experiences you describe are usually Soul Travel. It takes a very strong desire to do it, unless the Mahanta gives you a special hand. People must want to Soul Travel very much, otherwise they won't develop themselves spiritually for the journey. The worlds of God can overwhelm people who are not prepared for them.

So how can you get these dramatic inner experiences? Start by doing your spiritual exercises every night before you go to bed. Then, develop methods to remember your dreams better by using a tape recorder or taking notes.

Invent new ways of doing the spiritual exercises given in this book and the other ECK works. Make them more dramatic and appealing, to fit you personally.

After twenty years studying Soul Travel, I've not yet had a conscious out-of-body experience. Is there some kind of blockage within my subconscious? Would subliminal tapes help me?

It's good to be a Hound of Heaven, but not at all costs.

It's good to be a Hound of Heaven, but not at all costs.

We cannot force ourselves into a Soul Travel experience if that's not the best thing for us. Twenty years of trying is hardly a split second in eternity for Soul, but to us it represents much of our spiritual life.

Try backing off Soul Travel and master the dream state first. The dream state is just another aspect of Soul awareness, so it's the place to set a good foundation for Soul Travel.

Remember to pursue Mastership gently and not push. Instead of pushing to do Soul Travel, back up and learn all you can about the dream state. Both it and Soul Travel are doors to the same spiritual worlds. So experiment with your dreams.

If done right, you'll soon find yourself awake in the other planes without the need for Soul Travel of the popularly imagined kind: A big rocket that blasts you to the stars. Dreams are a gentler, equally effective doorway to spiritual exploration.

WORKING WITH AN INNER TEACHER

I have searched for almost thirteen years to find a path with an inner and outer teacher. I've learned a lot about Eckankar through books, but I feel frus-

*trated because I'm still not experiencing Soul Travel.
I wonder, Is ECK for me?*

I can appreciate your hesitation in regard to the
teachings of Eckankar. I had the same uncertainties
when I wrote to Paul Twitchell years ago as I looked
for a spiritual path.

Soul Travel is one of the foundations of
Eckankar. It ranges from the unmistakable state of
becoming aware of yourself in the Soul body, while
traveling on one of the neighboring planes, to more
subtle ones, such as having an insight into a concern
that previously seemed beyond your abilities to
solve.

The dynamic kind of Soul Travel is unforgettable
for anyone who is able to have it. It occurs through
the practice of the Spiritual Exercises of ECK.

How can I tell if the ECK Masters are real?

Once anyone has met an ECK Master, like the
Tibetan Rebazar Tarzs, physically or on the inner
planes, there is no further question that he or she
is a real being.

But not everyone has earned the privilege.

It is interesting to note that when one first steps
onto the path of ECK, he may have a number of
experiences that give proof of Soul's existence
beyond death. He is also shown the reality of the ECK
Masters of the Order of the Vairagi.

Then, over the years, he unfolds. Sometimes he
does so without recognition of his expanded state of
consciousness. His inner and outer experiences reach
a new level, but his awareness of this is nonexistent
until a radical change occurs in his everyday life.
This jars him in the awakened state, and what he

*The dynamic
kind of Soul
Travel is
unforgettable
for anyone
who is able
to have it.
It occurs
through the
practice of
the Spiritual
Exercises of
ECK.*

discovers is often unsettling. His experiences have toned down and interwoven themselves into his everyday life.

INNER AND OUTER MASTER

I've been a little scared of meeting the Outer Master. I'm afraid I will do something stupid in front of you and fail an important spiritual test.

The ECK Masters will not embarrass anyone who really wants to reach God-Realization. They well remember their own trials as they struggled to reach the mountain of God.

They are usually so down-to-earth and matter-of-fact that people immediately feel comfortable with them, as they would with an old friend.

I hear about the Mahanta, the Living ECK Master in Eckankar. Who and what is he? What is his function?

The Mahanta, the Living ECK Master is the spiritual leader of Eckankar. He is the spiritual guide for those on the path of ECK.

Sometimes people don't understand the role of a spiritual guide—whether it's Christ, or the Mahanta, or Buddha, or the leader of a church somewhere who has a very definite, direct connection with the Holy Spirit. So let me explain.

Over all creation is the creator, God, whom we know as Sugmad in the ancient teachings. The name doesn't make any difference. The creator is one and the same. The Voice of God is the active force that goes out and was responsible for the actual creation of all the universes. This Voice of God is what is known as the Holy Spirit. Or sometimes the Spirit

The Voice of God is the active force that goes out and was responsible for the actual creation of all the universes.

of God, the ECK, the creative force, or whatever. But it's a neutral force. It simply obeys or does the will of the creator.

Now a true spiritual master is in tune with the Voice of God. A human manifestation that people can see and understand. In that role, his will is that of Divine Spirit. And that's all.

In Eckankar this divine force works both in the Outer Master and also through the Inner Master. That means those on the path of ECK have the additional benefit of a Master who can come to them in the dream state and teach them there. Or sometimes by direct Soul Travel. Sometimes through contemplation. The Inner Master is there, working when the individual sleeps, or prays, or meditates, or contemplates. And the Outer Master is out here to provide the books, the discourses, and to give talks and things of this nature. But the Outer and Inner Master are not two separate things—they're just two different aspects of one being who serves the Holy Spirit.

This divine force works both in the Outer Master and also through the Inner Master—they're just two different aspects of one being who serves the Holy Spirit.

In his physical body, the Mahanta, the Living ECK Master is like everyone else and can only be in one place at a time. In the Soul body, however, he is like the air that you breathe. He is everywhere. As the ECK, he can easily be with you and thousands of others in the very same moment.

To put it another way, you can think of the Inner Master, the Mahanta, as a body and yourself as one tiny cell within his body. Millions of other cells are in it too. The Mahanta is always with all the cells within his body, whether they are in his toe or in his head.

The sole purpose of the Mahanta, the Living ECK Master is simply to help Soul find Its way home to God.

I'm not a very emotional person, but every time I see a picture of you or read certain things about you, I cry. Why is this?

It is Soul recognizing the Mahanta. This makes Soul happy. Out here, it explains why you cry.

I've noticed you do very little to sway others toward your ideas or even the Eckankar teachings. What is the spiritual reason for this?

People expect a lot of flashy speeches, but the Living ECK Master purposely keeps things on an even keel. It is all too easy to sway people's emotions with the right words so they make a decision to follow ECK against their will.

It's a spiritual crime to do such a thing.

A part of the seeker's test is seeing beyond the outer personality of the Living ECK Master. Eckankar is for the simple and pure of heart, for truth does not make a whole lot of sense to the intellectuals of society.

A part of the seeker's test is seeing beyond the outer personality of the Living ECK Master.

WHY DO THE ECK MASTERS SERVE?

What is the secret of becoming a Master? Why do it at all?

Someone once had an interview with a number of ECK Masters. She wanted to know why they served God. All of them began their reply with: "Because I like to . . . "

In addition, she learned that each did what he could do best. This was the secret of their Mastership and service to God.

The ECK Masters are agents of God whose only concern is to bring spiritual upliftment to each individual who is ready for it. At times this mission has been very difficult.

About three thousand years before the Christian era, the ECK teachings were taught openly in Egypt by Gopal Das. Severe persecution by the followers of the main religion, as well as by proponents of astrology, forced the Nine Unknown ECK Masters to submerge the teachings.

For almost five thousand years since then, the ECK Masters have worked quietly in the background, bringing spiritual upliftment in whatever way possible, even though not as direct as Eckankar.

How Is the Mahanta Chosen?

How were you chosen to be the Mahanta?

My training began several lives ago. In this life, I was put into the stern training of strict schooling as a youth, to prepare me for my mission in this cycle of time.

A number of people are being tested all the time to become members of the Vairagi Order of ECK Masters, which they must be before they are next in line for the Mahantaship. But first, they have to go through all the Eckankar initiations leading up to that level. One who to become the Mahanta is told of his chosen role when he is an adult, but then years of silence may follow as he goes through even stricter training.

All this is necessary for him to overcome the heavy resistance that he will meet from the negative force later in his duties as the spiritual leader. God appoints the Mahanta, and his predecessor announces him to the world.

There are many ECK Masters of every race. Men

God appoints the Mahanta, and his predecessor announces him to the world.

and women of all races belong to the Order of Vairagi. God makes no distinctions between age, race, sex, or creed. Neither does the Mahanta, the Living ECK Master. He serves all people with complete love.

JOURNEY TO MASTERSHIP

Sometimes I think it would be lonely to have total awareness—all alone, learning but never reaching an end, a home. There are days when I long to be rid of the lower worlds, but other times I am not sure that I would be happy. If you don't mind, would you please tell me when you reached the point in your life where you knew for sure that you wanted to continue learning into infinity and why. Also, what would one's goals be once he gained total awareness?

Actually, the Mahanta saw my deep desire for truth. He led me step-by-step because of my willingness to follow him. This led eventually to an experience told in my autobiography *Child in the Wilderness.*

It was on a bridge, with a stranger, that the limitations of my lower self were torn away. I felt alone, exposed, and afraid. And this was during the experience of God-Realization! Also in my book I treat some of the misconceptions that people carry about God Consciousness.

Service to God is life; anything less is nothing.

My goal now is simply to serve God. There is nothing else to do. Service to God is life; anything less is nothing.

What are the stages of growth in the higher spiritual levels? What's the relationship between the Master and spiritual student when the initiate gets closer to Mastership?

By the time one receives the higher initiations in ECK, most of the communication between the Living ECK Master and initiate is done through the inner channels.

One of the stages that we come to is learning to work in harmony with all life. This sounds too pat, too flat. But when we can see the Mahanta in all we meet—can see the Light of ECK in the eyes of people passing us in the street—then we can only give love in return to all life.

One of the stages that we come to is learning to work in harmony with all life.

To qualify for Mastership, Soul must know discrimination in Its love. Warm love for our dear ones, charity (detached love) for the rest of creation.

No one has the capacity to love all life without injury to himself. That is the purpose of discrimination. The ECK Masters practice detachment, but this does not mean lack of compassion. Nor does this mean interfering in somebody else's affairs.

Perhaps the hardest part of my duties is picking up a letter from my desk where someone asks relief from a crushing weight of karma and I know that it must be worked through. There is no shortcut available to him.

Of all those who work in the spiritual field, some are able to move quietly and cooperatively among people, while others generate a storm of controversy and disruption wherever they go. Why is that, all Souls being equal as the spark of God? There is always more to learn about acting as a vehicle for Divine Spirit—what it means and how it's done.

The ECK Masters work strictly through the spiritual hierarchy. That is step number one. They are not in competition with each other. They know their common mission is to serve the great Sugmad, as God is called in the ancient teachings. Secondly, they do so in harmony, nurturing the plus factor, the building element in all they do.

Tests of the Masters

Sometimes the tests in my life get so hard that I wonder if I'll ever make it to Mastership. Did the ECK Masters really have to go through things like this?

Life requires that Soul have every experience. No thought or deed is ever lost—but all is recorded in the Book of Life. Thus Soul learns to have compassion and charity, and to give service to other beings.

The spiritual giants have suffered the edge of the sword that wounded the heart, leaving them to cry in despair to God to give them a reason for their anguish.

When the trials are done and Soul is aware of Its relationship with God, then immense love and compassion are the reward.

The greater our consciousness, the more deeply we feel the slights of neglect, lack of consideration, and abuse by people who use our good nature against us. But there is a turning point where the Wheel of Fire, which is slavery to karmic destiny, loses its power over us. Henceforth we emerge from the fog of unknowing and travel freely in the sparkling lands of ECK.

The Masters in ECK are in a state of vairag, or detachment. It is a state of consciousness that is won the hard way, but when the trials are done and Soul is aware of Its relationship with God, then immense love and compassion are the reward.

You cry with the grieving in their sorrow, laugh with the joyous in heart, sit in silence to listen to the heart of someone who has touched the hem of the Lord. You are an inspiration to the weak, a solace for the broken in spirit. Thus you are a saint, a shining light to all who enter your circle of influence.

GLOSSARY

Words set in SMALL CAPS are defined elsewhere in this glossary.

ARAHATA. *ah-rah-HAH-tah*   An experienced and qualified teacher of ECKANKAR classes.

CHELA. *CHEE-lah*   A spiritual student.

ECK. *EHK*   The Life Force, the Holy Spirit, or Audible Life Current which sustains all life.

ECKANKAR. *EHK-ahn-kahr*   Religion of the Light and Sound of God. Also known as the Ancient Science of SOUL TRAVEL. A truly spiritual religion for the individual in modern times. The teachings provide a framework for anyone to explore their own spiritual experiences. Established by Paul Twitchell, the modern-day founder, in 1965. The word means "Co-worker with God."

ECK MASTERS.   Spiritual Masters who can assist and protect people in their spiritual studies and travels. The ECK Masters are from a long line of God-Realized SOULS who know the responsibility that goes with spiritual freedom.

GOD-REALIZATION.   The state of God Consciousness. Complete and conscious awareness of God.

HU. *HYOO*   The most ancient, secret name for God. The singing of the word HU is considered a love song to God. It can be sung aloud or silently to oneself.

INITIATION.   Earned by a member of ECKANKAR through spiritual unfoldment and service to God. The initiation is a private ceremony in which the individual is linked to the Sound and Light of God.

LIVING ECK MASTER.   The title of the spiritual leader of ECKANKAR. His duty is to lead SOULS back to God. The Living ECK Master can assist spiritual students physically as the Outer Master, in the dream state as the Dream Master, and in the spiritual worlds as the

271

Inner Master. Sri Harold Klemp became the Mahanta, the Living ECK Master in 1981.

Mahanta. *mah-HAHN-tah* A title to describe the highest state of God Consciousness on earth, often embodied in the Living ECK Master. He is the Living Word. An expression of the Spirit of God that is always with you.

Planes. The levels of existence, such as the Physical, Astral, Causal, Mental, Etheric, and Soul Planes.

Satsang. *SAHT-sahng* A class in which students of ECK study a monthly lesson from Eckankar.

Self-Realization. Soul recognition. The entering of Soul into the Soul Plane and there beholding Itself as pure Spirit. A state of seeing, knowing, and being.

The Shariyat-Ki-Sugmad. *SHAH-ree-aht-kee-SOOG-mahd* The sacred scriptures of Eckankar. The scriptures are comprised of twelve volumes in the spiritual worlds. The first two were transcribed from the inner planes by Paul Twitchell, modern-day founder of Eckankar.

Soul. The True Self. The inner, most sacred part of each person. Soul exists before birth and lives on after the death of the physical body. As a spark of God, Soul can see, know, and perceive all things. It is the creative center of Its own world.

Soul Travel. The expansion of consciousness. The ability of Soul to transcend the physical body and travel into the spiritual worlds of God. Soul Travel is taught only by the Living ECK Master. It helps people unfold spiritually and can provide proof of the existence of God and life after death.

Sound and Light of ECK. The Holy Spirit. The two aspects through which God appears in the lower worlds. People can experience them by looking and listening within themselves and through Soul Travel.

Spiritual Exercises of ECK. The daily practice of certain techniques to get us in touch with the Light and Sound of God.

Sri. *SREE* A title of spiritual respect, similar to reverend or pastor, used for those who have attained the kingdom of God.

Sugmad. *SOOG-mahd* A sacred name for God. Sugmad is neither masculine nor feminine; It is the source of all life.

Wah Z. *WAH-zee* The spiritual name of Sri Harold Klemp. It means the Secret Doctrine. It is his name in the spiritual worlds.

273

274

FOR FURTHER READING AND STUDY*

The Mahanta Transcripts Series
Harold Klemp

The Mahanta Transcripts are highlights from Harold Klemp's worldwide speaking tours. He has taught thousands how to have a natural, direct relationship with the Holy Spirit. Here are aids to help you to a deeper spiritual understanding.

Journey of Soul, Book 1
You are about to make a giant leap forward on this, the last leg of your long journey home to God. This book guides you toward a personal understanding of the nature of Soul, the possibility of past lives, how to overcome the fear of death, and the spiritual potential of dreams.

Our Spiritual Wake-Up Calls, Book 15
When God calls, are you listening? Discover how God communicates through dreams, the people you meet, or even a newspaper comic strip. Learn how you are in the grasp of divine love every moment of every day.

The Spiritual Exercises of ECK
Harold Klemp

This book is a staircase with 131 steps. It's a special staircase, because you don't have to climb all the steps to get to the top. Each step is a spiritual exercise, a way to help you explore your inner worlds. And what awaits you at the top? The doorway to spiritual freedom, self-mastery, wisdom, and love.

The Living Word, Books 1 and 2
Harold Klemp

These timeless writings can help you discover the power and the presence of divine love in your life. Learn, through stories and techniques, how to plan for and achieve tangible spiritual growth.

*Available at your local bookstore.** If unavailable, call (612) 544-0066. Or write: ECKANKAR Books, P.O. Box 27300, Minneapolis, MN 55427 U.S.A.

There May Be an
Eckankar Study Group near You

Eckankar offers a variety of local and international activities for the spiritual seeker. With hundreds of study groups worldwide, Eckankar is near you! Many areas have Eckankar centers where you can browse through the books in a quiet, unpressured environment, talk with others who share an interest in this ancient teaching, and attend beginning discussion classes on how to gain the attributes of Soul: wisdom, power, love, and freedom.

Around the world, Eckankar study groups offer special one-day or weekend seminars on the basic teachings of Eckankar. Check your phone book under **ECKANKAR**, or call **(612) 544-0066** for membership information and the location of the Eckankar center or study group nearest you. Or write **ECKANKAR, Att: Information, P.O. Box 27300, Minneapolis, MN 55427 U.S.A.**

☐ Please send me information on the nearest Eckankar center or study group in my area.

☐ Please send me more information about membership in Eckankar, which includes a twelve-month spiritual study.

Please type or print clearly   BK6A

Name _____
          first (given)   last (family)

Street_____ Apt. # _____

City _____ State/Prov. _____

ZIP/Postal Code _____ Country _____

ABOUT THE AUTHOR

Sri Harold Klemp was born in Wisconsin and grew up on a small farm. He attended a two-room country schoolhouse before going to high school at a religious boarding school in Milwaukee, Wisconsin.

After preministerial college in Milwaukee and Fort Wayne, Indiana, he enlisted in the U.S. Air Force. There he trained as a language specialist at Indiana University and a radio intercept operator at Goodfellow AFB, Texas. Then followed a two-year stint in Japan where he first encountered Eckankar.

In October 1981, he became the spiritual leader of Eckankar, Religion of the Light and Sound of God. His full title is Sri Harold Klemp, the Mahanta, the Living ECK Master. As the Living ECK Master, Harold Klemp is responsible for the continued evolution of the Eckankar teachings.

His mission is to help people find their way back to God in this life. Harold Klemp travels to ECK seminars in North America, Europe, and the South Pacific. He has also visited Africa and many countries throughout the world, meeting with spiritual seekers and giving inspirational talks. There are many videocassettes and audiocassettes of his public talks available.

In his talks and writings, Harold Klemp's sense of humor and practical approach to spirituality have helped many people around the world find truth in their lives and greater inner freedom, wisdom, and love.

International Who's Who of Intellectuals
Ninth Edition